Jeff McCallum

THE SMALL
BUSINESS
Success
MINDSET

A GUIDE TO FAST SMALL
BUSINESS GROWTH

The Small Business Success Mindset

ISBN-13: 978-1-990476-12-9

Published by: Expert Author Press
https://www.expertauthorpress.com/

Canadian Address:
36 Rockwood Street
Ottawa, ON K1N 8L7, Canada
Phone: (604) 941-3041
info@expertauthorpress.com

Tabel of Contents

To my wife Julie & kids Byron, Jeffrey, Amy, and Jordan. You are my rock.

Introduction

Forget past mistakes. Forget failures. Forget everything except what you're going to do now and do it.

— William Durant

I saw my first career coach earlier this year after being a successful business owner for over three decades.

When I told those in my inner circle about my decision to seek this service, they immediately responded, *"You, Jeff, are seeing a career coach? You started several successful businesses and sold two companies for millions of dollars. Why would you need a career coach?"*

Being a successful business owner was a massive part of my identity for most of my adult life. I almost didn't know how to do anything else. But now, at 61, I'm no longer interested in starting another business. I know how much time, dedication, and energy it takes to do so, and my sights have significantly shifted toward other ventures. However, the lessons I've learned along the way are not something I would want to sit on. There is so much to be said about how to build and grow a business, and what good would it be to keep it all in my aging mind? I needed to figure out what to do with the knowledge and wisdom I've acquired over the years, thus my desire to seek a career coach.

"So, what brings you here?" she asked during our first session.

I thought long and hard about how I wanted to respond to her. I knew I didn't want to start another business; I just wanted to repurpose what I'd learned in a more summarized, efficient manner through what I know best: Talking.

"I want to help people grow their businesses, and I need some direction on how to do it in the right ways," is what I landed on.

"Do you see yourself running seminars or writing a book to share those experiences?" she asked.

I told her I'd already engaged in seminars as a speaker, discussing business-related things I felt were helpful. I also considered writing another book, as I'd already published two books a few years before. I was open to doing all those things again but on a larger scale.

I started seeing her once a week, and the more she learned about me, the easier it was for her to know why I was so interested in sharing my experiences with others to help them become better entrepreneurs.

"You, Jeff, make up the 1% of the population that utilize both sides of their brain. There's one side of you that's extremely creative and the other side of you that is incredibly business-savvy. You have an incredible work ethic, and you think differently than most people—what most people think of as success is not your definition because, to you, success has no limit. You are always willing to go above and beyond because there's always more to achieve."

I'd say that was a pretty good definition of me. I love music and business... I guess those two interests make up my right and left brain.

"Maybe you need to speak to others similar to yourself but who have not yet tapped into what they're fully capable of," she continued.

This resonated with me deeply. I always knew I wanted to do more with my life. I didn't want to settle for the bare minimum. When you think of the greats of this world, like Richard Branson, Steve Jobs, and Bill Gates, they didn't settle for the bare minimum either. They worked tirelessly to get to where they were, and I did as well. Not that I can compare myself to the most remarkable business people to ever walk this earth, but I did pretty well.

What if I could speak to others like me, who have so much ambition, hunger, and drive to do more but are getting in the way of themselves by doing too much of the wrong thing?

The more we talked, the more I realized my near-future career path would be consulting with either novice business owners starting their journey or current business owners on the verge of failure. The more I divulged aspects of my past—the hard times, the good times, and the pivotal times—the more I realized I needed to map this out chronologically. Start reflecting on those times as an angsty teen with so much passion and little direction, as a young adult jumping from job to job trying to find my place in the world, to an aspiring business owner who tackled new opportunities and ran with them until they became successful. I learned lessons from these experiences and wanted to share them.

Fast forward to today, and I'm writing this book. And if you're anything like me and consider yourself the top 1% of people in this world who want to learn more, do more, and achieve more, this book is for you.

I'd like to show you how you can build your business the right way the first time so you can live the life you've always dreamed of. **Believe me, it may be easy to get into business, but I can assure you it's damn hard to keep one alive.** In this book, I will walk you through the vital lessons you must learn to build, grow, and sell your business for millions of dollars.

In Chapter 1, I'll recount how I became the entrepreneur I always aspired to be, the paths I took, the confusion I encountered, and the people who helped me get to where I needed to be. Then, I'll teach you what it takes to build a business with a solid foundation in terms of your branding, the people you hire, and the systems you put in place in Chapter 2. By Chapter 3, we'll dig into the most important lessons about being in business–handling the money. After Chapter 4, you'll understand who should be in your leadership team and how they can help you develop the life you've always envisioned. Chapter 5 is all about the work-life balance you need to achieve to keep things moving in the right direction and help you avoid burnout. Chapter 6 delves into how I replicated the systems I put in place in my first company to create a successful business in a quarter of the time. Chapter 7 discusses the process of selling a business and Chapter 8 reveals how my life has been after selling my first business for millions of dollars. All the way through, you'll discover the mindset you need to achieve all this and more.

It is possible if you hunger to become a successful business owner with fool-proof systems, impeccable employees, raving fan customers, and millions of dollars in the bank. If you are in business now and things aren't going how you'd like, this book is for you. While hard work is a critical factor, it is not the only one. It's not even the most important one. You just have to be willing to make a few fundamental changes, and there is no better time to start than now.

Becoming the Entrepreneur

*If you don't make plans for yourself, guess what others
have planned for you.*

— Jim Rohn

If you had asked me as a child what I wanted to be when I grew up, I would have told you I wanted to be a rockstar. Rocking out on stage with my bandmates, colourful, glowing lights strobed over the cheering crowd, filling up the stadium as large as the Colosseum. *"Jeff! Jeff! Jeff!"* The crowd would scream after my two-minute guitar solo that some would equate to the great Jimmy Page. The final song would end, and we'd say our goodbyes with sweat dripping down our faces, only to be met with all 80,000 of them screaming, *"Encore! Encore! Encore!"* They couldn't get enough.

You see, I'd always been a dreamer. These fantasies played out in my head repeatedly in my childhood and adolescence. My mother played the violin and piano, and she had put my brothers and me in music lessons at a young age. So, I inevitably thought a career in the music industry would be where I found myself.

Then, as time passed, reality did not seem to be lining up with my vision. The one-in-a-million odds of making it big as a rockstar would not land me the lifestyle of my dreams. I wanted a wife and children, and touring the country did not support the life of a family man. This volatile lifestyle was not the structured one I needed. I realized I just wanted the freedom that life would provide. The freedom to be creative, to be a rogue. I didn't want to live by anybody's rules but my own.

It became painfully apparent that this type of freedom took a lot of money. If I ever wanted to enjoy the finer things like fast cars and private jets, I needed hundreds of thousands of dollars in extra cash. I was excited about the prospect of making tons of money, but at the same time, it felt incredibly daunting. I had barely graduated from high school and had no idea what I wanted to do with my life.

So, I didn't become a rockstar. I became a lost boy.

Navigating Life in the 80s

It was the early 80s, and I had bills to pay. I was living in Northern Canada, and my father helped me get a job at a gas plant. The money was decent, and I soon found myself on a new career path: becoming a working stiff. As I sat in the break room, watching everyone smoke and complain about their lives, I realized I still had dreams. There was no way I could punch the clock and do the same thing year after year until retirement. I felt trapped in a deadened job, and I did not want to kiss my freedom goodbye.

To be honest, I did not have the mechanical aptitude to be in any sort of trade. I'd always been too outgoing for that type of career and always felt I could do more. If I stayed there another year, I'd be more unhappy.

One long weekend, I went south to visit my brother Rob and vented to him about the predicament I was in. He recommended that I read, Pulling Your Own Strings by Dr. Wayne Dyer, and told me to take hold of my life. In his book, Dr. Dyer claims that many people stay in unfulfilling jobs because they fear change and choose to remain stuck in their present experiences. However, people can master their fate if they learn strategies and tools to be responsible for their outcomes and prevent victimization and manipulation by others.

Until that point, I had never been a reader. This book piqued my curiosity and became the first of many to change the trajectory of my life forever.

While staying with him, I couldn't help but notice the huge collage of random photos taped onto his refrigerator. *"What's that?"* I asked, confused. *"That's my dream board,"* he confidently announced. *"It's a visualization technique that can help you turn your thoughts and dreams into action."*

He then recommended a second book, The Magic of Believing by Claude M. Bristol. Reading it made me bask in the possibility of increasing my income and influence while improving my peace of mind through positive affirmations. I quickly learned that focused thinking not only enhanced my career, it also helped my personal life.

Inspired, I quit my job at the gas plant and moved to Kamloops, where I sub-contracted to a taxicab company called Yellow Cabs. I thought it would be the best opportunity to learn how to operate a business, improve my communication skills, and get to know the locals in my city. After a few months, I quickly noticed that weekends were mainly reserved for the drunk twenty-somethings celebrating a night out on the town, while weekdays were taken up by drunk individuals blowing their social assistance cheques on rides and booze.

It was hardly the inspiring or fulfilling business I envisioned, but it taught me how to run my own business.

A few years later, I sold the taxicab lease and worked in service and sales at a pest control company back north. My boss lived in Vancouver, so I only saw him occasionally, leaving me responsible for how I did things. I've always been good at talking to people, and this job helped me develop that skill and build trust with prospective clients. I did a consistent gig for a few years, but it wasn't checking any boxes of being my long-term career.

When Rob told me about his new carpet cleaning business that he had gotten into, I thought it was a pretty smart idea because most people had carpets in their homes at the time. No one else had been doing it, either. I immediately became interested, and Rob asked if I wanted the guy's number who sold him the franchise. His name was Bob Burnham.

When Jeff Met Bob...

Jeff McCallum, John Childers, and Bob Burnham

Bob was a successful entrepreneur from Toronto who moved to Vancouver in the 80s, started a carpet cleaning company, and then franchised the hell out of it across Canada.

I first met Bob in the early 90s, and by that point, he had several franchisees who were thriving, including my brother Rob. I'd just moved to Victoria with my wife and three children, and when Bob suggested I buy a franchise, I was on board. Within that first year, I owned a carpet cleaning business, too. Bob became a mentor I could go to for advice, but he soon became a really good friend. I admired his values, zest for life, and undeniable work ethic. Most of all, he did not see the world the same way everyone else did. This made him approach business from a completely different angle. Whatever everyone else was doing, Bob seemed to do the opposite. I knew I could rely on him to lead me down the right path and make the right decisions to become as successful as he was.

Bob was even more into personal growth and creating your destiny than I was. He would recommend books and encourage me to seminars and conferences. All this new learning led to mind-opening conversations and significant shifts in perspective. We would always be talking about how every problem contained infinite possibilities. We'd take note of any great idea we saw, and whenever someone else was successful, we'd study what they had done, break it down, and apply anything we could to our business. One of our favourite sayings was, *"It's all made up,"* meaning that anything we see in the world and accept as fact is someone else's hallucination that they brought into reality.

Not even a year into the business, I received a call from a property management company that asked if I could extract water from an apartment building after a major rainstorm flooded dozens of basements in Victoria. I quickly realized that I could make more money extracting one basement than I could carpet cleaning the entire week, so I made several calls to other property management companies to see if they required my services, which they jumped on immediately. I spent that entire weekend from morning until night extracting basements, and I had made more money in those few days than I had the whole year.

Most business books will tell you the same thing: Follow the money. So, that's exactly what I decided to do. Needing some advice and reassurance, I called Bob. *"What if I could help people restore damage in their homes from fires and floods? I don't think there are a lot of companies doing that right now."* I enthusiastically said to Bob. *"It looks like it will be one of the fastest-growing industries right now."*

And that's precisely what I did. With Bob's help, I re-vamped the carpet cleaning business by turning it into a restoration service business. As soon as I started offering these services to clients and was making more money than ever before, I knew this was what was going to make me the successful entrepreneur I'd always dreamed of being. I delved into restoration exclusively and took the plunge to start something of my own.

That was when ABK Fire and Flood Restoration was born. We took what we knew worked well from the carpet cleaning industry and got busy creating.

So, are you ready for your first couple of lessons?

It's Time to Start Making Plans For Yourself

When I reflect on those early years at ABK, I think of a young man who finally stopped letting other people make plans for him and started making plans for himself. I began to live by my rules and built my empire. The dream of living on my terms finally began trickling into the real world. I could have continued to work in jobs that didn't fulfill me solely for the paycheque and stability, but I knew that wouldn't make me happy in the long run. I knew I needed more out of life. I knew if I would spend most of my life working, it had to be something I enjoyed. It had to be cultivated by me and for me. It had to fit the lifestyle I wanted.

So, I didn't become the next Jimmy Page or fill up the 80,000 seats of the Colosseum. What I did become, though, was a successful entrepreneur who made a fortune along the way and sold his business for millions of dollars, and I think that deserves rockstar status in its own right.

If you're reading this and are thinking this sounds like you, then you're probably one of those people born to do more. I know the feeling and how it can eat at you when you feel like you aren't living up to your potential and could be doing something more with your life.

Do you hate your current job? Are you unhappy with your current lifestyle? Do you have a desire to create your schedule? Run your own business? Chase your dreams? Grow an empire? If this is you, here's your reminder to stop letting others make plans for you and start making plans for yourself.

It takes drive, commitment, and dedication. It takes a hunger to work smarter and harder than ever. It can be the most rewarding opportunity you could ever do for yourself, but only if you do it the right way.

Jeff McCallum with Def Leppard

Identify the Niche, Act Quick, and Then Run With It

Bob didn't become a multimillionaire because he opened a carpet cleaning business but because he opened that business when the carpet cleaning industry was ripe for the taking. It was a niche that others hadn't taken a hold of yet, leaving a gap in the market for Bob to fill. Bob saw how lucrative it was and took it to another level by franchising it.

When I identified restoration as another niche that could dominate the market, I knew it would work to my advantage solely because it was another up-and-coming industry with very little competition in my surrounding area.

Jumping on a niche business opportunity is one way to ensure your business will thrive, but timing is also essential. You don't want to have the idea and sit on it. If you find a viable niche opportunity that could work as a business and competition is low, you want to get that going right away before someone else beats you to the punch. We all know that one person who says they thought of x-y-and-z product/service before a so-and-so person/company did it. It doesn't matter if you thought of it. It's a moot point and means nothing if you don't act on it. Read some business books, attend a few seminars, get a business coach, and make it happen!

Once you've made your plan, determined your niche, and implemented it within a decent timeframe, it's time to set up your foundation. In the next chapter, I will show you how you can build your processes the right way the first time around so you can replicate them seamlessly.

Take Inspired Action

Feel-good stories are nice to read, and the warm fuzzy feeling is good until it wears off. How do you keep the inspiration flowing? You must work at it and constantly feed it with positive thoughts and energy. Have you ever noticed how negative everyone around you can be? It's human nature to whine and complain. We love to commiserate, but we get uncomfortable seeing someone leaving the pack and setting a trail to success. We want them to stay wallowing in the mud with us. As you start to think and act differently, other people will try to hold you back, telling you that it will never work. That's why you must work on your mindset every day.

First, you have to take control of your destiny. This sounds like a huge step, and it is, but it does not have to be complicated. It can be as simple as spending some thinking time daily, focused on what you truly, deeply desire. I'm not talking about what society says you're supposed to be, do and have because that is the recipe for pain and misery. I mean digging down deep and uncovering your dreams and setting goals.

One simple thing that I bet every successful person you know does in some way, shape, or form is writing out their goals and reviewing them daily. Get a notebook or create a file on your phone to do this every morning when you wake up and every evening before bed. Write out the list of things you want in your life and spend time thinking about them every day. This will create an energy of possibility in your life and drive your awareness toward making these dreams happen.

Look what happened to me after I saw my brother Rob's vision board on his fridge! For that matter, make yourself a vision board. All it takes is doing searches online and in magazines for images of your dreams. Cut them out and paste them on a piece of bristol board. You don't have to do anything fancy. I once heard a speaker say you should keep your vision board beside the TV. That way, you must put your dreams aside every time you watch it!

Become a Life-Long Learner

I was never much of a reader until my brother recommended those two books to me on that momentous visit to him one long weekend. After meeting Bob Burnham, I started reading all the time. I'd ask him what he was reading and then go out and get it. Pretty soon, we were both recommending books to each other.Most people stop learning after they finish school. They get into a rut, doing the same old job and complaining about how boring it is.

Don't let this be you. Start reading non-fiction books. Ask someone you admire to recommend their favorite book. Google famous people's reading lists. Get a library card. The library is such a fantastic free resource, and they have an app, so you don't even need to go in to borrow books. What's even more incredible is the wealth of audiobooks you can listen to while walking or driving. How great is it to kill two birds with one stone? You can make a lot of headway into a book if you listen to it every time you get into the car. Here's a little pro tip. Most authors go on podcasts to promote their book. Seek out these interviews because you always get deeper insights from their lessons learned. My other favourite hack is to listen to the audiobook while reading the physical book. The two modes of learning seem to implant the material deeper in my brain.

Become a better communicator. If there is one thing, you will notice throughout this book is how important it is to communicate with customers. Not only will it win you business, but it will create raving fans and get you repeat customers and referrals. There are all sorts of courses you can take. Look for a local Toastmasters club. There are multiple clubs in every city, and they will teach you the art of public speaking at a very low cost. Look out for courses offered in the community. These can be a great place to set out on your learning path.

I honestly believe there is no better investment than one you make in your learning. I am constantly investing in myself by hiring coaches and joining mastermind groups to surround myself with people building the things I want. You must protect your mindset by only exposing it to those supporting positive growth. That's why finding places where like-minded people hang out is critical.

"Clarity happens 10 seconds after you take action."
–Jeff McCallum

The next thing you know, you can spot opportunities everywhere you look. One person's problem is an entrepreneur's next million-dollar idea. Start keeping track of these ideas and do your research. See what kinds of solutions exist and how satisfied people are with the results they provide. When you find something nobody solves, start asking around to find out what people would pay to solve the problem. Maybe this is the start of a new business for you or a new product or vertical in your existing business. However, a great business is not built on ideas alone. They must have a solid foundation to deliver consistent customer service and make good money. The next chapter covers the foundations you need to build your business right.

Building a Solid Foundation

*Great businesses are not built by extraordinary people but
by ordinary people doing extraordinary things.*

— Michael Gerber

When ABK opened its doors in 1991, I had a newfound optimism that I had never felt before. It was the first time I felt like I took the bull by the horns to cultivate the future life I envisioned for myself and my family. I saw a niche opportunity and went for it. I wasn't the lost boy I had been in my youth, following everyone else's plan but my own because I was unsure of what I wanted or needed. I needed this business to thrive, and knew I could do it if I did the work.

It started as a one-man show. I was doing my labour, marketing, and bookkeeping. I had one van, managed my schedule, and hustled as much as possible to build my clientele. It was not a walk in the park in the beginning. I put my blood, sweat, and tears into this company and put a lot of pressure on myself to ensure I did my best. I understood that running a business would be a lot of work, but I didn't realize how many different roles and tasks I would have to deal with, and to be honest, I wasn't good at most of them.

In my first year of business, I barely made $78,000 gross and had worked myself to the bone. I made several mistakes trying to do my bookkeeping and accounting, and my marketing efforts were less than ideal. I knew there had to be a better way.

I decided to attend some business seminars with Bob to learn more about improving my current situation, and two speakers impressed me: Michael Gerber and Brian Scudamore. Gerber wrote *The E-Myth: Why Most Small Businesses Don't Work and What to Do About It*, and he believed that you could scale any business if you treat it like a McDonald's franchise by having your systems in place from the beginning. Scudamore, the founder of *1-800 Got Junk*, built an empire by solely collecting people's junk and implemented Gerber's concepts into his business early on. If Scudamore could become a millionaire by hauling away junk, there was no reason why I couldn't do the same, repairing fire and flood damage.

So, I picked up a copy of The *E-Myth* to delve into the ins and outs of running a small business by treating it like a franchise. Then, I read it two more times. I became obsessed. Gerber had figured out how to break through any small business's growing pains; three lessons, mainly, made the most significant impact.

The E-Myth Takeaways

Business owners spend too much time working in their businesses and not enough time working on their businesses, and that's a huge part of why most small businesses fail within the first five years.

Gerber states that we become three different types of people when we start a business: The entrepreneur, the visionary and the dreamer. There's the manager, the executor. And then there's the technician, the doer. The problem is most small business owners wear the technician's hat 70% of the time while wearing their entrepreneurial hat 10% of the time and managerial hat 20% of the time.

So, can you call yourself a true entrepreneur if this is the case?

When you first get into business, you will inevitably be wearing several hats in the beginning to hit the ground running. While this approach is necessary to get your initial cash flow, it's not sustainable and will eventually run you into the ground. It wasn't my place to be the technician in my company for the long term. I was meant to be the entrepreneur, the visionary.

Today, whenever I speak at different functions about my business success, I always get a lineup of people afterwards who want to take me to lunch to get my advice on their business ventures. In those conversations, the person will reveal that their business is struggling and on the verge of failure. Whenever this happens, I first want to know how involved they are and the task they're doing. Most of the time, they're the technician and neglect their entrepreneurial duty.

They have difficulty letting go but can't accept that it's causing them more harm than good. My first advice is to tell them they must spend time working on their business instead of in it. It worked for Gerber, Scudamore, myself, and thousands of other business owners who faced a similar outcome.

This is the first step, and the sooner you understand and implement this key advice, the sooner you'll see changes occur.

Takeaway #2:

If the purpose of going into business is to free yourself of a job, then you need to create jobs for people who are much better at doing those tasks than you are.

Gerber reveals that once you recognize your life's purpose is not to serve your business. Still, the primary purpose of your business is to serve your life, you can then work on your business, rather than in it, with a complete understanding of why you must do so.

You are not good at everything, and there is no way you can do all of these different roles yourself. The quicker you realize that the easier your life will be. By attracting the right people and assembling a dedicated team who believes in your values, you can rid yourself of the tasks that have taken up all your time to be the entrepreneur in your business. Finding like-minded individuals who buy into your vision and mission is your ticket to a prosperous destination.

I took this lesson and expanded my team rapidly over the following years. I subcontracted work to others, eventually getting people on the payroll when I had the appropriate overhead. I had my full-time technicians take on more jobs and continued to subcontract work to contractors, painters, and other labourers when I couldn't get more people on the payroll. I did this until we were a business comprising several departments with systems in place being managed by different people.

I created a business with a punctual, reliable, positive, enthusiastic, and respectful team. With a team sharing my values, I built a multi-million dollar company that ran like a well-oiled machine, and I could watch it all unfold from the sidelines.

Takeaway #3:

If you consider your business a national franchise, start with one and implement the systems you'll need to replicate it eventually.

When Gerber says you need to set up your business like a McDonald's franchise and have the right systems in place from the very beginning, it isn't an exaggeration. Your systems have to be in order, or everything will fail. Sure, McDonald's may not have the best burger you've ever had. But for some reason, people have been flocking to McDonald's in the masses for the last 68 years. Why? Because you always know what you're going to get. It's consistent. It's the same every single time.

When you maintain that level of consistency in your systems, you receive that level of consistency in your results. That's why you can order a Big Mac anywhere in the world they will pretty much taste the same. The recipe for success for McDonald's was its impeccable systems, which allowed Ray Kroc to bring McDonald's from a boutique burger joint in San Bernadino to a worldwide sensation with franchises in almost every country.

There are three types of systems you will need to implement: hard systems, like the machinery or objects you're going to have your employees use, soft systems, like your ideas or concepts, and information systems, such as your training materials. Your employees need to be aware of and trained to use or apply each type of system to ensure consistency in your business. People work well when they have systems to follow, which means you can step back and let others do the work.

Build Your Processes So Good That You Can't Run Without Them

When I think back to those early days of ABK, I knew that to stand out from the crowd, I had to take Gerber's advice at face value and make the necessary changes to give ABK its own recognizable and respected identity. I had to provide customer service unlike any other company doing this type of work. A happy client means a lifelong client. A happy client turns into a referral machine. ABK had to be the best in the business regarding quality work and service. That became my vision, and to bring that vision to fruition, my first line of work was to build the processes, which included building the brand, the team, and the systems.

Build the Brand

ABK's brand had to exude professionalism and exceptional customer service, and the first step to achieve this was to create a sharp, professional logo. It consisted of a red A, a light blue B, and a purple K, followed by the bolded slogan, **We make it right again**. When people saw this logo, I wanted them to think *they could save my property and do it well!* The logo looked quite sharp against our white, shiny Chevy vans; it would be the first thing to attract the attention of passersby driving past us on the highway or walking by the properties we were working on.

Think about your current or future logo. Does this version of it encapsulate how you want people to view your brand? Do you think people would consider it memorable? Many people overlook the importance of a logo and how it can impact your brand. The colours and font you use can make a huge difference in how your company is perceived— Discordant colours or unprofessional fonts are one way to kill that. Think about it, would you ever trust anyone whose logo is written in Comic Sans font? I don't think so.

While your logo is a snapshot of your brand, nothing exudes your brand more than the faces behind it. The appearance and attitude of your staff mean everything, and they ultimately build your reputation for you. Think of an unruly and unkempt employee. Perhaps they have greasy hair and strong body odour, or maybe they're wearing a ragged Metallica T-shirt, sweatpants, and dirty shoes, and their truck is filled with garbage on the dash. Now think about someone who is the complete opposite. Maybe they have a professional uniform and a glossy truck and care about their appearance and personal hygiene. Which of these people are you likely to employ, and which one of these people would be respected by your clients?

There's no question that people are more likely to trust a person in a uniform and clean truck who seems to have their act together. Not only do customers instantly feel relieved that the right person handles their concerns, but it also dramatically increases their perception of your company and brand.

Having my brand exude professionalism and attaining the respect it commanded was paramount to me. That's why I decided if a person wanted to be associated with ABK in any way, they had to be the face of the brand. They had to show up in a clean uniform, a glossy truck, good personal hygiene, and a fantastic attitude. If they didn't wear the uniform when they came to work, they didn't work that day. If their van was filthy, they didn't work until it was cleaned.

The uniform doesn't have to be over-the-top, either. ABK's uniform consisted of a white golf shirt, black dress pants, and all-black shoes, and everyone was required to drive a company vehicle and keep it clean. These were the rules I wanted to implement early on to ensure our brand's image was never tainted. First impressions are everything. However, the brand is more than appearance.

Impeccable Customer Service Is the Key to the Kingdom

Early on, Bob noticed that I was good with people. He told me that this was one of my skills and that I should focus on putting this to use. Working for the pest control company taught me that sales was just a matter of finding out what people wanted and then agreeing on a way to give it to them.

Whenever people were unhappy, I loved to go in and see what their expectations were and where they were not getting met. By simply asking them questions and getting them to agree on what a job well done could look like, it was not hard to make them happy. So I went out to talk to clients and insurance companies to make sure that everybody was not just satisfied but delighted with the service that we were providing. I was always taking calls and getting back to people to reassure them that we were on top of their projects and that they were in good hands. That reassurance went a long way to maintaining happy customers who became repeat customers and provided many referrals.

When people thought about ABK, I wanted them to feel how we cared for them. We went above and beyond to make the moment right for them; they were our priority. That was the type of brand I wanted to be, and I wanted everyone to remember it. ABK's brand was all about professionalism and customer service: this is what made up the DNA of our company.

So, what is your brand? What aspects make up its DNA? How are you going to make your brand shine to the outside world? When people see your logo, are they interested in learning more? When people read your slogan, will they instantly know how you can help them? When people see your employees, do they feel comfortable and at ease? The brand is everything. Brand is how you market your company and give it a name for itself. The brand is how you build your reputation and success.

Build the Team

I've had a lot of crappy jobs in my life, but I did those jobs knowing it was just the starting point and that I would be moving out of that job and getting someone else to fulfill the role. I also did those jobs with the mindset of the bigger business that I was creating rather than the dollars that I was earning for the hours I worked, work that was done with the vision of creating ultimate customer satisfaction.

I had to think like the customer and understand their psyche. When I thought of customer service, I would think, *What does it look like when I show up at the door? How do I make them feel confident I've got their back and will do a good job for them?* I understood immediately that first impressions were extremely important. A customer's judgment was based on how I showed up at their door, who I was, and the job I would do. If I wore dirty clothes, jeans, or a T-shirt that looked bad, what kind of confidence was I inspiring? Likewise, if they saw my truck and there were coffee cups on the dashboard, papers and bills and candy wrappers all over and spilling out the door, could they be inspired to think I would treat their house respectfully?

When a person undergoes loss due to a fire or flood, it's a very emotional time for them. People's homes are an extension of who they are. They represent family and relationships, hopes and dreams, and a lifetime of memories. Our first contact with the client is a very intimate moment that few people seem to understand. Somehow I got this intuitively. I knew that I had to inspire trust and confidence in the homeowner. This was just part of my personality and something I was naturally good at. I loved talking to people and making them feel comfortable.

This industry does not attract people from refined backgrounds or with high levels of education or worldly points of view. I couldn't rely on them to understand how to behave in every customer interaction. They needed to be trained to behave the same way every time to uphold the image of ABK. This only existed in my mind, which I inherently understood and knew how to portray through my actions and behaviours. I had to find a way to ingrain this in my employees.

I quickly learned that there would be a lot of instruction and training in getting people to serve customers the way I did.

As a one-man show driving around in my truck, I learned what to do with employee number two. The dude got in my truck and filled it with a pungent aroma of body odour. The internal dialogue did not last long since I had to contend with this guy in a confined space. There was no way that I could expose any customers to the offensive smell. I had to tell him that his personal hygiene was less than satisfactory, and if he wanted to keep his job, he needed to do something about it. We worked it out, and he kept working for me.

When it was time to build the team even further, I immediately understood which roles I needed to drop from my day-to-day list of tasks so I could free up some time to hire, train, and work behind the scenes to keep the ship moving in the right direction.

I hired a professional bookkeeper to take care of the finances, and helped me keep a clear record of how we were doing at every moment. The moment I did this, those small, tedious mistakes I kept making became a distant memory, and I consistently received an accurate picture of our small strides. I then took on a few technicians and provided them with their vans so we could take on more clients in different locations.

Getting more hands on deck helped me grow quickly and freed me up to do more hustling and start putting the right systems in place.

I did not have the technical know-how that many people on my team have. That's why once you recognize your strengths, you want to focus on maximizing your use of them and outsourcing all the other areas where you don't excel. Once I did this, I could see where my attention was needed and let others lead with their strengths.

Build the Systems

Since I ran ABK alone for several years, I already had several hard systems, like the machinery and tools used to provide our services. But now, with more people on board, I needed to ensure I had enough of them to distribute to all my staff and that every van was equipped with the same products.

We needed to have some baseline protocols around behaviour that conveyed my vision and standard for customer service, and these became the soft systems that I put in place to ensure that the average standard of customer service was always present. But beyond that, I needed clear information systems to get those messages ingrained in their heads from the minute they came on board. With some research, I came across a training program that would change the trajectory of my business from that moment on, Steve Toburen's *Winning on the HomeFront.*

Toburen created a series of audio tapes to train people in what he called Service Engineering, a principle that focuses on how work is delivered rather than how the actual work is done. He indicates that 80% of how the homeowner decides if your company has done a "good job" or "bad job" is based on their relationship with the person doing the work in their home. Any Tom, Dick, or Harry could come in and restore a property, but are they building relationships with customers? Are they making them comfortable, easing their fears, and mitigating their concerns? Are they creating customer cheerleaders who actively promote their business for its impeccable work AND exceptional service? I wanted my employees to do all those things, and I knew this would set us apart from the rest.

Whenever an employee would join the team, their training involved going through the tape series and learning the methodology. We also discussed these methods every week at our weekly meetings, which I liked to call our weekly mosh pits. Employees would bring up examples of successful interactions and client success stories where they felt they exceeded customer expectations. They would also bring up situations where they were struggling and needed help. because everyone on the team was so well-versed in the methodology, there were always a lot of helpful insights offered. Very often the person with the problem walked away with the solution and implemented it within the same day.

Once Your Processes Are Solid, It's Time to Market, Market, Market!

Marketing, for me, is about showcasing all the hard work done and becoming an integral part of the community. It's the step where you've solved problems and now must broadcast your solutions to the world. Marketing is a vast term, and its definition varies for each business. It's crucial to recognize its broadness and the many offerings in the market. Some folks learn the hard way, like a guy I spoke to who went through eight marketing companies, facing disappointment each time.

Investing wisely in marketing is key. I had read a lot of books on marketing and we did a lot of it ourselves. Our professional image was key. Sometimes we handled our marketing and advertising internally, and other times we'd bring in marketing professionals. Ultimately, My experience was that having a great reputation in the community was the best marketing. We always made sure to have a detailed schedule of activities from firetruck pull events with the fire department to advertising in various community initiatives. Having a suite at the events center, although a $25,000 annual investment, proved to be a strategic move. It built confidence among potential clients, especially when they saw our name aligned with other reputable local businesses.

Reciprocity became a crucial element. For example, having a suite at the event center provided exposure and allowed me to foster relationships with adjusters and brokers. It wasn't just about handing out hockey tickets; it was about picking up the phone and communicating, creating moments of truth, and ensuring a seamless job.

The marketing approach should align with what you're good at. It meant being on the phone often and communicating extensively with clients and potential customers. Joining Chamber of Commerce meetings, participating in networking events, and being part of the business community proved effective.

Nailing down the essence of marketing, especially for us, involved active participation in the business community. This included attending Chamber of Commerce events, builder shows, and charity initiatives. Every business, regardless of its field, has associations and conventions—being part of these networks is crucial. Attending these conventions and taking up sponsorships roles paid off really well for us. Another really powerful move was putting on educational seminars for adjusters and brokers. It's a great example of reciprocity because, while they really appreciated our efforts, we got a lot of business from them.

Breaking Down the Client Visit

With the help of Toburen's *Winning on the HomeFront,* I implemented the procedures each employee of ABK would have to follow before, during, and after the client visit. Let's briefly break down what each part looks like.

Before the Visit

Staff were required to call the homeowner to confirm the appointment, ensure they were home, let them know they were on their way, and ask where they should park. Staff were to arrive in full uniform, accompanied by a meticulously clean truck and an organized set of tools. When they stood at somebody's doorstep they were to stand 3 feet back and have a business card ready in hand. I was always really big on the idea of asking permission for everything when you're in a homeowners house and never taking things for granted. This gave them a sense of control and they could feel that we really cared. Everything was about ensuring the homeowner's sense of confidence and safety.

During the Visit

Staff were required to knock on the homeowners' door and step three feet back to maintain distance. They were to introduce themselves and ask if they could come inside. Always asking for permission builds positive moments of truth with the homeowner.

Once inside, staff were to cover their shoes with plastic booties and ask the homeowner to direct them where the work was needed. If staff must return to the homeowners' house to provide additional services after the first visit, they would schedule it with the homeowner the same day. If the homeowner was feeling uneasy or something went wrong, we found that it could usually be solved by over delivering on customer service and good communication.

At the end of the visit, the staff were just to communicate someone would be in touch with him for scheduling if they needed to come back to the house. To help the homeowner feel a sense of closure, we had them complete a satisfaction survey to ensure they were content with the service provided and outline any concerns or improvements they wished to be made. We started doing this long before insurance companies demanded satisfaction forms. As a special thank you, we would give a gift basket of local products to the homeowner, creating yet another positive moment of truth. These carefully thought out gestures all made customers more understanding and forgiving if things didn't go according to plan.

After the Visit

Staff were required to contact dispatch when they completed a job. A project manager or dispatch would call the homeowner to ensure things went well and they were satisfied with their results. If there were any concerns, they would book another appointment to finish the job to satisfaction. Testimonials from satisfied clients were a powerful tool, creating a book of endorsements that spoke volumes about our reliability and excellence. This approach was not just a tactic; it was a success catalyst.

Take Inspired Action

Which Hat Are You Wearing?

If you are in business now, we need to get you to stop working in your business and start working on your business. If you are just starting up, let's look at how you can build your business like a franchise. It all starts with asking yourself what hat you're wearing. Are you being the technician and doing the work? If so, how much of your time is that taking each day and each week? If other people work for you, how much time are you managing them? Are you constantly putting out fires? As an entrepreneur, are you looking for new business opportunities? Can you see ways to do what you are currently doing more efficiently? You want to understand how much time you spend in the three roles (the entrepreneur, the manager, and the technician) from *The E-Myth*.

Understandably, when you start up, you will need to wear all three hats, but knowing that as an entrepreneur, you want to move towards wearing the entrepreneur hat. Once you know how much time you spend in each role, schedule time every day and week to work on your business instead of in your business. During those times, you are not allowed to do technical work or spend time putting out fires for your team. You are working on new business ideas and innovative ways to deliver the results you deliver better. Ensure your entrepreneur time goes in your calendar and is sacred.

Outsource Everything You Aren't Good At

If the only thing you can do well and enjoy is the service your business delivers, you will be stuck in a job for a long time. Maybe owning a business is not your calling. However, if you can scale your business by hiring people to do the time-consuming work for you so that you can move to work on the business, you must make that shift as soon as possible. Make a list of what you are good at doing and what you need to find someone more skilled than yourself to do. Begin looking for ways to contract out the jobs you aren't good at. Hiring contractors may make more sense, or you may find that bringing someone in-house is the most cost-effective way to proceed. You'll want to run the numbers on this and move forward with the most cost-effective approach for the current size of your business.

Create Your Systems

Consistency is the key to success in business, and systems are the key to consistency. As you replace yourself as the technician with contractors and employees, you must ensure that they deliver the same results you delivered in the same way. This involves systems for everything. Look at all the processes involved in delivering your product or service to your customers and get to work writing down every step. Create a manual with all your hard, soft and information systems. This manual is the evidence that your business is becoming franchise-like.

Tell the World You're in Business

Speaking of consistency, how will you consistently let people know they can buy from you? Marketing takes planning. It's not something you do when you need more clients to pay the bills. You do it week after week, month after month. Identify where your customers hang out and ensure they find you there. If your ideal customers are members of a certain organization, join it and attend their meetings. Make sure you're on the social media platforms they are active on. From there, be helpful. The point of your marketing presence is not to sell, sell, sell. It's to let people know you understand their issues and can help. That's why it's such an asset if you can see the world through their eyes.

Take Your Customer's Perspective

This is something that can be a little tricky but will reward you richly if you do it well. Get into your customer's shoes and look at the whole situation through their eyes. What are they most frustrated with, and what are their biggest fears? For our customers, it was trusting their family heirlooms in the hands of rough and careless labourers. I had to think about all the places where they would feel insecure and shut down. I wanted them to feel confident that we would provide silk glove service in a dirty industry and that Grandma's antique vase would not get dropped or splattered with paint. How can you reassure your customers that they can trust that you have their back? This is a crucial element of your brand and part of the promise you want to make to your customers.

Evaluate Your Brand

When discussing branding, most people immediately think about their website, colours, and logo. While these things are important, they are only the outer surface of what your brand represents. The ABK logo, tagline, uniforms and trucks represent the customer experience and quality workmanship that people could expect from our company. Ask yourself if your brand has a deeper meaning than your business card and logo. When people see your logo, what experience do you want to be associated with it? Your brand is your opportunity to make a promise to your customers as to why choosing you will make them happy. Think about McDonalds. The golden arches don't represent the best-tasting burger. They guarantee the burger you know and love, no matter where you buy it.

Make a list of everything your company does to provide an experience that customers can't get from any of your competitors. How do you deliver on these promises to ensure that customers experience this level of satisfaction every time? This is what makes up the heart of your brand. When you are known for your brand promise, you know that the outer shell of your colours, logo, and tagline carries clout in the market.

Ensure that Your Team is Living Your Values

When you can no longer work with every customer to make sure that they are having the experience that you want them to associate with your company, who's going to do it for you? When you have team members delivering to customers on your behalf, you must ensure they provide the same level of service with the precise experience that your brand promises. How do you ensure everyone who works for you exudes your brand's values? In our case, we did it through training courses and our weekly mosh pits. Every week I could see how well my team was living our values, have team members help others to provide better service and address any issues that might hinder our ability to keep our promise to our customers. Devise your system to ensure that your team is living your values and get it in place immediately.

Once you have a solid foundation, it's time to grow. This is the place where a lot of entrepreneurs get caught up. Hiring people and buying equipment looks like growth but may hold you back. It is important to focus on the finances and plan your growth strategically. In the next chapter, we'll address the biggest concern that most entrepreneurs I meet fail to handle.

Handling the Finances

Money, like emotions, is something you must control to keep your life on the right track.

— Natasha Munson

Businesses exist to make money, so every entrepreneur needs to ensure their business is doing so. The fact that I talk to so many business owners only to find out they are not making any money tells me there is a huge disconnect here.

When I was working to build ABK from the ground up, I did my books. While I made several mistakes, it helped me understand the basic principles of operations and cash flow. While many people understand these basics, they don't take the time to ask the fundamental questions: How is the money coming into me? How do I know I'm getting paid? How am I paying everybody? How do taxes work? What are source deductions?

When starting as a small business entrepreneur, you will ultimately do most things yourself and need to know how to answer these questions. If you don't answer these fundamental questions initially, you might encounter very complicated circumstances come tax season. As a new business owner, that's the last thing you want to deal with. In this chapter, let's go over some of the challenges you may run into and how to handle your finances correctly to save yourself from stress in the long run.

Understanding Your Overhead and Cash Flow

Paying attention to your overhead and cash flow is an important aspect of being an entrepreneur. Money in and out may seem obvious, but many business owners ignore the basics of operations. They take on too many costs too soon and don't have the overhead to cover it.

The Real MVP Is Your Bookkeeper

Your first line of business is to hire a bookkeeper to ensure you can handle all of the hard costs associated with being in business. If you don't have one, here is your public service announcement to hire one as soon as possible. And no, it shouldn't be your wife, husband, or Aunt Lucy. It should be a professional bookkeeper who can keep you accountable and has the skills to show you when you're working beyond your means. They are essential to your growth and will help you take on more leaders at the right time.

Your bookkeeper is the one who can tell you where you are in your business at every given moment. Knowing how much is coming in and going out is extremely important. A bookkeeper can provide you with the nuances of the finances to help you understand where exactly your money is going and how it is coming in, so you have an accurate picture of the profits you're making and the possible growth steps you can make next.

If your monthly expenses, such as your building lease, equipment, car payments, employee salaries, and contractor pay-outs are not being covered by your revenue, you need to spend the time reevaluating your current situation and determine how to increase your cash flow.

If you aren't making money, it may be time to consider why. Are your employees being properly trained? Are you utilizing each role to its full capacity? Are you following the systems you put in place? With all these things considered, you may need to evaluate your pricing to make sure you're charging enough. These things must be working in harmony for growth to occur.

Navigating Financial Challenges

At one point early in my growth, I found myself with payment flowing out of my accounts faster than I was able to collect on my receivables. Several sleepless nights and persistent financial stress ultimately led me to explore unconventional solutions. I discovered a factoring company that would pay me 75% of my receivables upfront, if I was able to insure those receivables. Just this discovery alone was enough to put my financial fears to rest and see that every problem has infinite solutions. While we did not end up engaging the factoring company, this experience taught me the value of being resourceful during tough times. It is often times of challenge that lead to the discovery of alternatives you wouldn't have considered otherwise.

The Stress of Receivables

Managing receivables can be the most stressful aspect of business. Balancing a substantial amount owed to you with existing financial obligations can be overwhelming. Understanding this process and discovering unconventional solutions, like factoring companies, has proven invaluable despite the challenges.

The stress peaked as accounts receivable piled up, and the complexity grew with the number of jobs. Balancing payments to suppliers, managing payroll every two weeks, and dealing with a relentless stream of financial obligations became overwhelming. The strain intensified as we utilized a line of credit to navigate these challenges. The importance of meticulous diligence in collecting receivables, especially from project managers, became evident. Details often overlooked in completing projects added to the delays in receiving payments.

Strategic Payment Terms

Determining payment terms is crucial and can vary based on the industry. For instance, with the insurance industry, you had to be ready for anything. Sometimes it could take weeks to get paid for emergency work and restoration, and putting everything back together would take even longer. Negotiating a 50% down payment after receiving the go ahead on a project and making sure it is approved is critical to maintaining cash flow. Aligning it with your business model and industry norms is essential.

When structuring payment milestones, consider tying them to project completion. This ensures a fair and transparent process. While this example fits the insurance industry, every business may have a unique payment schedule approach. For instance, large jobs might warrant an advance from the client, especially if it aligns with the nature of the work. We found it helpful to maintain a work-in-process spreadsheet to stay on top of the progress of all our jobs. A soon as a job was logged in as a new job it went on the list and we used the work-in-process sheet as a way to see where we were at with our projects. While it is not really necessary from an accounting standpoint, I found it helpful for budgeting because I could see what revenue would be coming in over the next few months.

External Contractor Dynamics

As ABK expanded, the need to hire external contractors was essential to manage the uptake in projects. Still, managing accounts receivable became increasingly complex and added more financial pressure. After several missed payments and miscommunications, developing clear contracts and maintaining effective communication with these external contractors became essential.

Establishing mutual agreement on payment terms with external contractors allows them to grow alongside your business and enables you to take on larger projects as your company expands. Failing to align with subcontractors on these terms can lead to challenges when tackling more significant ventures.

Dependence on Adjusters

An additional layer of complexity arose from our dependence on adjusters and their processes. The adjuster's role in billing and seeking payment from the insurance company introduced delays. We discovered that the intricacies of adjusters' internal processes could significantly impact the speed at which we received payments. This interdependency highlighted the importance of effective communication and collaboration with all stakeholders in the payment chain.

Strategic Collections Focus

In the hustle of business growth, it became clear that effective collection strategies are as crucial as securing new projects. Being proactive in managing collections emerged as a vital aspect of financial stability. This realization dawned during a particularly challenging period of rapid expansion, where increased workload led to more subcontractors, overhead, and, consequently, delayed payments.

The turning point occurred during one of the most stressful periods in my business journey. The company was flourishing, but the pressure intensified due to the heightened number of projects, subcontractors, and increased overhead costs. This boom brought forth a critical challenge—the delay in receiving payments, causing a financial squeeze.

To tackle this dilemma, we hired hired a person to focus on accounts receivable and why jobs were not getting paid. Her job was to bridge the communications gap and speed up payment. This level of focus turned things around quickly. This experience underscored the importance of adapting to financial challenges swiftly and decisively.

Revamping Policies and Procedures

The lessons learned during this period prompted a comprehensive review and revamp of policies and procedures. This included overhauling how projects were managed to ensure timely completion and payment. The emphasis shifted to training project managers to navigate the intricacies of project completion efficiently.

To maintain a proactive stance on collections, weekly leadership meetings were instituted. This platform facilitated a real-time assessment of project status and ensured that all aspects were completed for timely billing. The significance of constant communication and follow-up in the payment process was highlighted, preventing delays caused by incomplete paperwork or oversight.

The growth spurt, while advantageous, came with its set of challenges. The stress was compounded by having project managers overloaded with work. This led to a critical realization—the need for a balance between growth and operational efficiency. Acknowledging the potential pitfalls of rapid expansion, the focus shifted to streamlining operations and optimizing the workload to prevent undue financial pressure.

Daily Financial Check-Ins

It was always important for me to be able to tell where we stood financially on a daily basis. When we grew to a size that could support the role, an in-house financial controller who could oversee all the financials became the key to our success.

A fundamental practice emerged: daily financial check-ins. This simple yet effective routine involved regular conversations with our controller, and administrators. This facilitated a comprehensive understanding of the financial landscape, allowing quick decision-making. Work-in-Process became a key daily metric to ensure a clear picture of ongoing projects and their financial implications. These check-ins provided a holistic overview of our financial status, fostering confidence in decision-making and ensuring a proactive approach to any potential financial challenges.

How Financials Changed with Growth

At its inception as a one-man show, ABK made a whopping $70,000. By the second and third years, the business was gaining momentum, with revenues reaching the impressive range of $500,000 to $700,000. However, the turning point came around the fifth year, marking a consistent surge to $700,000 to $800,000 in revenue. Over the following decade, the figures reached new heights, making multiple millions annually. NorHaz followed suit, but because we'd been down the road before, it only took five years to generate millions.

The journey through this growth phase reinforced the importance of strategic financial planning, proactive collection strategies, and effective communication. The experience became a pivotal chapter, influencing the ongoing commitment to maintaining financial health and resilience in the face of business challenges.

Removing the Managerial Hat

The team at ABK knew that they had to follow these procedures every single time with every client. I would even call them part technician and part social worker because they were responsible for mitigating the client's emotions while completing the work. If they wanted to work for me, that is what they needed to do consistently, and it was on me to ensure it was being enforced.

As the business grew, it became more difficult for me to spend time training each employee to follow these systems and procedures while also trying to take on more new business. I loved building rapport with clients and establishing relationships with adjusters who could get us more new business. Still, it was hard to find the time to do all that while also training and coaching my employees to develop their mindset and embody the vision, mission, and values of ABK.

I had removed the technician hat entirely, but I was still juggling being the company's entrepreneur and employee manager. ABK was on an upward trajectory, but with the amount of growth we were experiencing, it was about time to reorganize the company and implement new practices. It got to a point where it wasn't working anymore, and I needed to get some leaders on board who could execute my vision and lead a team of people to do the same. It was ultimately time to develop my leadership team.

In the next chapter, we'll discuss how you can get the right people in the right seats to run your company for you, giving you more time to do the things you love and take your entrepreneurial spirit to the next level.

Developing the Leadership Team

*Incredible things in the business world are never made by
a single person, but by a team.*

— Steve Jobs

As the vision for ABK was unfolding before my eyes, it just made me hungrier for more. I had created customer cheerleaders promoting our brand to everyone they knew requiring our services, and customers recognized ABK as the best in business. Our clients were becoming referral machines, so much so that I didn't invest that much in marketing and advertising because the word-of-mouth referrals were so explosive. The last thing I wanted was for everything to come to a screeching halt because I couldn't keep up with the growth. I had to ensure every new employee wore a specific hat to fulfill the company's vision and mission. To do that, I needed more leaders to help me execute my vision.

Wearing Multiple Hats:
The Entrepreneurial Journey

Embarking on the entrepreneurial journey often means donning a multitude of hats. In the initial stages, you find yourself as the owner, the marketing guru, the sales expert, the finance whiz, and the HR specialist. That's a lot of hats, and each comes with its own set of responsibilities. It's like b eing the conductor of a one-person orchestra. However, as the business grows, there comes a critical juncture where wearing all these hats becomes impractical. This realization hit home for me during a challenging episode involving accounts receivable. Even a decade into the business, I juggled too many roles. The key becomes strategic delegation—passing on these hats to capable team members.

The Hat Inventory

Let's break down the five major hats: owner, marketing, sales, finance, and HR. Each broader category encompasses numerous sub-hats, making the entrepreneurial role a complex web of responsibilities. Under marketing, for instance, you may deal with branding, advertising, and public relations, and each requires a unique skill set.

The art lies in recognizing when to relinquish a particular hat. It's about understanding that you can't do everything as a business leader. Hiring the right people—or, as I like to call them, moshpit cheerleaders—is crucial. These are individuals who not only possess the skills needed for a specific hat but also align with the vision and culture of the company.

Delegation is not just about passing off tasks; it's about entrusting someone else with a piece of your vision. When hiring, whether it's a project manager or a financial expert, you're essentially taking off a hat and placing it on someone else. The transition requires trust but demands a keen eye for talent.

The Hiring Criteria: Matching Hat with Expertise

When bringing new team members on board, consider their expertise. If it's financial responsibilities you want to shed, hire someone with a proven track record in finance. The same logic applies to marketing, sales, and other facets of the business. Hiring someone who's qualified and fits seamlessly into your team is crucial.

The entrepreneurial journey is a delicate balance between holding onto the reins and letting go. Recognizing your limits, understanding when you've reached the capacity of a particular hat, and having the humility to seek expertise elsewhere are the hallmarks of effective leadership. It's not just about building a business; it's about assembling a team where everyone wears the right hats, and the collective synergy propels the company forward.

The transition from handling everything yourself to delegating involves recognizing when to let go of a specific hat. The goal is strategic delegation: finding the right people with the skills that resonate with the company's vision and culture.

Marketing, financials, HR, and all the other hats work harmoniously when the entrepreneurial leader can communicate and delegate effectively. Juggling these hats is an inevitable part of the entrepreneurial journey: it's a dance between taking charge and knowing when to pass the hat to someone else. Each hat represents a key aspect of business and the real art lies in orchestrating these roles to create a harmonious and thriving company.

Who Should Be On My Leadership Team?

A few members of the ABK Crew

Deciding what your leadership team should look like and whom it should entail is an important aspect to consider, and it all depends on how much you want to grow. If you are in a position where your cash flow covers your overhead and you have extra to invest, that investment should be put towards developing your leadership team. Their roles and titles will vary depending on how your company is structured. What matters is the freedom they will give you to remove parts of the managerial hat to free up your time to make moves as the business owner.

I knew I wanted to maintain a small business and have a few locations across my province. I wanted the financial freedom to spend my money, give back to the community, and spend with my family and friends. I was hungry to get there, and I knew that because the brand was thriving, the team was solid, and the systems were properly in place, I had the means to do so. But I also knew I didn't want to have a large corporation, hundreds of employees, and a headache to build that kind of empire. I didn't want my business to be my entire existence. I was comfortable with a small empire that made me millions. I also wanted to dip my toes into other side projects and passions that could make me an extra income.

Managerial Evolution: From Solo Entrepreneur to Strategic Leader

Early on in the business, my roles encompassed entrepreneurship and management. Marketing and overseeing the workforce fell under my purview, while a bookkeeper managed invoicing. I made crucial decisions, invested in new equipment, and maintained pivotal relationships. I actively participated in claims, trained the project manager, and occasionally handled claims personally. I considered myself the President of ABK, but I was more than that: I was a business owner, an entrepreneur, a labourer, a bookkeeper—pretty much a jack-of-all-trades.

My core team consisted of a bookkeeper, a few in-house technicians, subcontractors, and one woman with so many hats on that it would be difficult to give her a distinct title. She was the office manager and project manager, but she also prepped the receivables and payables for the bookkeeper. Since everyone was already working to their full capacity, I thought it might be time to fill more seats. I was interested in growing and wanted our brand to be viewed by the masses, not just by those perusing the phone book or by word-of-mouth referrals.

The In-House Controller

At the five-year mark, a pivotal move was made: introducing an in-house comptroller, whom I affectionately call a controller. This professional addition played a crucial role in financial management and laid the groundwork for future expansions. This role replaced the in-house bookkeeper role, as it extended beyond traditional bookkeeping and encompassed everything from invoicing to scheduling, showcasing the adaptability required in our industry. This period marked a transition from a singular focus on day-today operations to a more strategic approach to business development.

The Project Manager and Head Administrator

Shortly after, we added the Project Manager and Head Administrator roles, additions that were crucial for the day-to-day operations and overall management. The project manager assumed a second-in-command role and managed relationships with adjusters and brokers, which mirrored my responsibilities. I knew that if I trained the project managers to understand the importance of customer service, the implementation of systems, and the goals set in place to grow the company, they could be the ones to train the employees below them to do the same. To help facilitate organization after taking on more project managers, we implemented the Head Administrator role to oversee and schedule the project managers and technicians on jobs. The addition of the project manager and head administrator roles meant that I could partially remove the managerial hat and wear the entrepreneurial hat for the majority of the time.

The External Contractors

In addition to our core team, we also engaged external contractors, relying on sub-trades like electricians, plumbers, and carpenters for specialized tasks. The organizational structure during this period laid the groundwork for the subsequent transformation into a well-oiled machine.

The Vice President

A significant shift occurred in 2012 with the hiring of a Vice President who set the stage for more streamlined operations. As responsibilities were gradually delegated, the realization of the business's intrinsic strength unfolded.

Even before the official appointment of a Vice President, the focus had shifted from hands-on involvement to effective communication. The crucial role of phoning and maintaining open lines of communication became evident, emphasizing the importance of effective leadership.

By the end of 2012, I had a Vice President, eight project managers, dozens of technicians, a head administrator, an in-house controller, and a handful of subcontractors. With these people on board, ABK was making millions annually.

More Time On Your Hands Means More Opportunities

When I decided to develop the leadership team in the early 2000s, a lot of the time I had spent being so invested in the business's day-to-day functions was freed up. For someone hungry and motivated by delving into new opportunities, that time was best spent educating myself and taking risks.

Bob and I continued to attend seminars together and read books about business because we were insatiably hungry to learn more. Education was what got me to this point in the first place. If it weren't for those books I read while still unsure what I wanted to become, I wouldn't be here with a thriving multi-million-dollar business. I wouldn't have the outlook I have on life today. I am always on a quest to learn more and apply the teachings of others to my personal and professional life.

While I was working on building ABK, Bob was still in the world of franchising. When I told him I was interested in a new opportunity, he suggested starting a painting and carpet cleaning business with him that we could franchise. In 2001, BurnMac was born. By that point, putting BurnMac together felt like a walk in the park. Bob had 20 years of experience in the franchising world, and the two of us combined had the knowledge and expertise to build a solid infrastructure that followed the same principles and methodology as our other businesses. Within nine years, we had four franchisees, one of which stayed with us until the end.

Bob Burnham and Jeff McCallum

In 2003, Bob approached me with the idea of creating an online publishing company to help business owners write and publish their books. Online book publishing was relatively new at the time, and knowing Bob's thirst to capture a niche opportunity at its onset, he didn't want to overlook it as a fleeting idea. So, he asked me if I wanted to be a part of it.

I was initially apprehensive about joining him since ABK was growing so rapidly and BurnMac was in its early years of existence. Still, I couldn't say no to opportunities if I understood them to be viable and lucrative. In 2006, Bob and I wrote the first book we published under Expert Author

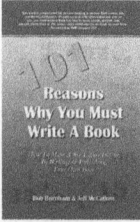

Publishing called *101 Reasons Why You Must Write a Book: How to Make a Six-Figure Income by Writing and Publishing Your Own Book.* We published it on Amazon, and it did pretty well solely because we hustled to get people to read it.

We reached out to everyone in our inner and outer circle, knowing that if we wanted our names to be known, we had to go out and hustle. Bob taught night classes at the local college on how to write and publish a book and I continued to look for places we could speak to find people interested in publishing a book. He initially did much of the push, speaking at many local venues and collaborating with other marketers.

By 2009, we decided to close the doors on BurnMac. We just couldn't keep up with the demands of another business any longer. ABK was growing exponentially, and my son Jeffrey had come on board to help manage the operations. Jeffrey being there helped take a massive load off of me, as I was still working with Bob part-time on the publishing business. And by that time, Bob had decided to make Expert Author Publishing his full-time gig.

In 2012, we published a second book called *Change One Belief*, and the demand for publishing books online grew significantly, eating up much of my time. This part-time gig demanded more of my time and required me to travel, pulling my attention away from ABK. Since ABK was growing exponentially, I decided that the best thing to do for my energy and well-being was to follow the money. Sometimes, saying no to opportunity is necessary for your growth.

The next chapter concerns work-life balance and the necessity of being a full-functioning business owner.

You probably hear about this often, but many overlook it, especially when we're dedicated to our work. Neglecting it for too long can have devastating consequences, and if I were you, I'd steer clear of that before it's too late.

5

Avoiding the Complacency Trap in Your Professional and Personal Life

When you recover or discover something that nourishes your soul and brings joy, care enough about yourself to make room for it in your life.

— Jean Shinoda Bolen

Complacency can be thought of as many things: the killer of dreams, the death of the soul, the enemy of progress. Think of every successful entrepreneur you idolize, and they've most likely spoken about the complacency trap. It's what every successful entrepreneur fears in their lifetime: the feeling of not progressing, bettering yourself, not moving forward or changing. It's the opposite of satisfaction, and the one thing that can prevent one from rising from good to *extraordinary.*

I had always had this mindset to learn, do, and achieve more. I had this thirst for knowledge and hunger for success at a very early age, and I carried that with me throughout my adolescence and adulthood. I had gone into this because I wanted financial freedom to live my way and do everything I wanted to do. Be a family man, dedicated husband, and successful entrepreneur. Live a rockstar lifestyle, travel to interesting places, and meet interesting people. Fast forward a couple of decades, and there I was, creating and co-creating successful businesses.

As an entrepreneur, you aim to make your business bigger, better, stronger, and faster. You want to be the best business person to ever live, and you won't stop until that happens! Most of us who have the drive and ambition to think this way will do it, and they will put hours and hours into their business to make it thrive. And then when it gets to a certain point, they stop. They stop devoting the hours to learning new methods, implementing new procedures, improving their culture, or cultivating the right team. They stop looking for new ways to market themselves, become a better leader, or strengthen their brand from competition. They get... complacent. This complacency not only prevents them from bettering themselves as an entrepreneur, but also trickles into their personal life—a routine that is unchanging and stagnant.

A certain mindset is crucial to grow a successful business while simultaneously raising a family and being the best version of yourself. It's difficult, yes, but not impossible. A mindset like this can be cultivated with the right set of practices.

Avoiding the Complacency Trap

When my wife and I booked our first trip in over two decades, it became abundantly clear what I had been missing out in my personal life.

What?! Your first vacation in two decades? you ask. Yes, it's almost embarrassing to say it out loud. After spending weeks in Italy cruising down the coastlines, indulging in its marvellous cuisine, and relaxing in the warm waters of the Mediterranean Sea, it occurred to me that I probably should have been doing this ages ago. Would the business still have thrived if I took a vacation here and there? Most likely. Would everything crash and burn if I stayed home during a cold? Probably not.

I will admit it was hard to step away from ABK initially. I'd never been five thousand kilometres away from the business with zero insight into what was happening. Even when I was pursuing other ventures, I still had a good look into ABK from the sidelines. It took a while to shake this feeling of not knowing, but I had a team handling it. I had just taken on a Vice President, for Pete's sake! I could trust them to run the business just fine while I took a vacation for a few weeks.

That summer in Italy changed everything for me. I came back a new person with new priorities so I could avoiding falling prey to the complacency trap, professionally and personally. This was the balance I encouraged myself to practice, but there were a lot of rules I had to set in place in order to make it happen naturally.

The more I practiced living a balanced lifestyle, the bigger, better, faster, and stronger I became and the farther I steered from falling into the complacency trap. And now, after years of perfecting this balance, I am writing to teach and encourage others to do the same.

Prioritizing Self-Care

The McCallum Family

Most of us go into business to have the physical freedom to live by our own rules and the financial freedom to spend our money as we please. We take the time to build our brands, teams, and systems to have a foolproof infrastructure that can run without us so we can spend more time doing the things we love. But do we end up doing the things we love?

I sure as hell did the things I loved professionally. Building a business from the ground up was invigorating, so much so that I believe it became an obsession. When everything ran as it was supposed to, I channelled all my energy into new businesses and replicated the model from scratch every time. I spent years educating myself on new practices, methods, and systems; I read every business book and attended every seminar to be the best.

But after years of hustling, I wasn't physically, emotionally, and mentally in the place I wanted to be. It was almost like I had to break the tether to my business so that I could focus on the other parts of me that used to bring me joy. I had become complacent about these vital aspects of life, and it wasn't until that trip to Italy that I was able to recognize it and make some changes.

Prioritizing Your Physical Well-Being

Taking a step back from working in the business to work on the business comes with many perks, like watching your kick-ass team take your business to new heights than you ever thought could be possible. But as a business owner, many things must be done behind the scenes. And often, that occurs on the phone or at your computer while sitting at your desk. You're no longer moving around from site to site, lifting heavy things and burning calories daily. You're instead pretty inactive, and that inactivity can start to creep up on you relatively quickly.

When I was engaged in all three companies, I didn't prioritize what I would eat during the day, so I'd resort to takeout or fast food every day. I'd have pretty restless nights since work was all I could think about and would wake up feeling groggy. I had always been active, but even that was starting to slip.

When I decided to take action, I did it in full force. I carved out time into my busy schedule and made it happen. I got a gym membership and worked out every other day, prepared my breakfast and lunch the night before, and ensured I went to sleep and woke up at the same time every day.

I felt the results of this almost immediately. After a couple of weeks, my energy levels rose, the dark circles under my eyes faded, and the brain fog dissipated. After a couple of months, I started to lose body fat and gain muscle, meal prepping became a part of my routine, and I felt better than I had in years.

Today, at 61 years old, I've maintained this routine and am in the best shape of my life. I feel better than I did at 20. I never could have imagined that would be the case. But with a little bit of dedication, it happened.

You can't rely on motivation alone. It has to be as much a part of your life as working on your business. You're going to wake up and go to work so you can make a living, and you're also going to wake up and take care of your physical well-being. There's no way around it, and the only way to make it work is to discipline yourself to do it. After a bit of routine, it will become second nature, and I'm telling you, you'll never be able to go back to a sedentary lifestyle because you'll feel too good. And when you feel that good, you'll work even harder, and it won't be as difficult.

Prioritizing Your Mental Well-Being

When I started working out and eating better, my mental health improved drastically. If I missed a day, my body and mind immediately felt different, and I started to realize how much better I felt by fueling my body and giving it what it deserved.

When you improve your physical well-being, your mental well-being will simultaneously improve. It's no wonder they say diet and exercise are one of the key prescriptions to alleviate depression and anxiety. The endorphins your body produces during exercise elevate the serotonin and dopamine levels in your brain and keep your brain healthy. Eating healthy, balanced meals is the receipe for necessary for improved hormone regulation and gut health, and with good gut health comes good mental health. The gut is your second brain, and when it is in a funk, your mental health can be drastically affected. Don't undermine the gut-brain connection.

I also noticed that I didn't make room for negativity. Whenever I would hear people complain or rant about things, especially about politics or religion, I immediately felt my attitude and energy become more negative. It's crazy to feel the shift in that energy so quickly, but it became a part of when I had another state of mind to compare it to.

Walking through the world with a positive attitude and energy made me a better person and nicer. I'd always been known as a compassionate, friendly, and positive person to begin with, but I no longer wanted negative energy around me because I just didn't like how it made me feel. I decided I would form my own opinions about things from personal experience and exploration and not rely on the opinions of others. When others would go into their daily rants about things that pissed them off, I would tune them out, knowing I didn't need their take on things to ruin my day, especially if we had differing opinions. People spend so much time defending their opinions and wasting energy fighting with people about them.

This became one of my training techniques when I brought new people on board at ABK. Sometimes, clients would go on rants about something that pissed them off, and because our line of work is almost like social work, you'd have to listen to them. And you wouldn't always agree with their take on things. I'd ask my staff, *"Do you want to spend all day trying to defend your opinion and cause more tension? Or would it be best to nod your head and appease them so the job can get done and the client is happy? Would you rather be right or successful?"*

Knowing what to spend your time and energy on is crucial when developing better mental health. There's a lot of terrible stuff going on in the world. It's important to be informed, for sure, and avoid misinformation and opinions of others so you have an understanding of what the true facts are. But it's also important to know when to disconnect and tune it out. We can't change everything in the world, but we can determine how we react and deal with it going forward.

Now, I like to live my life in the positive. I enjoy being around positive people who know how to engage in important discussions without draining the life out of me. I try my best to partake in a lifestyle that allows me to build on that energy to prioritize my mental well-being continuously.

Prioritizing Your Emotional Well-Being

What's the difference between your mental well-being and emotional well-being? Aren't they the same thing? While they're both aspects of psychological health, they are indeed different. According to Mindful Health Solutions, mental well-being is formed by rational thinking, good decision-making, and managing difficult situations. In contrast, your emotional well-being is managing your moods and feelings, such as stress, anger, sadness, and joy.

We may not always have great outlets to channel those emotions when they arise. And often, it's hard to recognize how and why we feel it. Getting to know what triggers your emotions is an important first step, and identifying the unhealthy coping mechanisms you usually take to alleviate those emotions is the key to changing them.

Historically, when I'd feel stressed or angry, I'd dive into work to distract myself, but at night, these emotions would make me toss and turn, and I'd have a hard time shutting my brain off. Whenever I feel these emotions overwhelming me, I channel them into working out, going for walks, and playing the guitar. I have more open discussions with my wife about what's happening, whereas before, I'd keep them buried inside. It took a long time to get there, but in my quest to improve my self-care, I read many self-help books to understand the psychology behind all of this. When I started creating coping mechanisms to deal with these emotions, they helped me keep them at bay.

Prioritizing Your Spiritual Well-Being

We all navigate this world with our belief systems. If you're religious or spiritual, these beliefs help make sense of the world and the many unexplainable questions surrounding our universe. As you try to balance your professional and personal lives, leaning into your religious beliefs or spiritually is a great way to keep you grounded and grateful for everything you've built around you.

I practice mindfulness daily and focus on being in the present moment and getting into my flow state. When I was younger, I was so focused on my future that I forgot to live in the present, and a lot of time passed. Paying attention to my present state helps me acknowledge my mental and emotional well-being and keeps me in tune with my feelings at every moment. The practice of mindfulness has helped me become more grateful, grounded, and aware of the ever-changing nature of the world we live in.

Regardless of who or what you believe in, whether it's a deity or yourself, prioritize it so you can remember the driving force behind everything you do and achieve.

Become A New-and-Improved You

There is no question that avoiding the complacency trap and prioritizing my self-care made me a better businessman, husband, dad, friend, and person. I wish every day that I had done it sooner because it would have saved me a lot of stress, but sometimes difficult circumstances are what enable these lessons to stick for good. It's like an alcoholic finally deciding to become sober: they have to get there on their own.

I understand the difficulties of putting yourself first when trying to build your empire, but it's important to think of your future self in those moments. Imagine a future where you are burnt out, tired, inactive, unmotivated, and complacent. Does this sound like someone who can successfully run a million-dollar business? Is that the version of yourself you want to become?

Start small. Go for a 10-minute walk after a meeting. Opt for a healthy meal for lunch instead of a cheeseburger. Read a book on a topic you're interested in learning. Go on YouTube and find some quick workouts you can do anywhere.

Pick up the guitar and jam for 15 minutes. Play golf with a buddy. Call a friend to see how they're doing. Book a therapy session if you're having a crappy day. Travel more. Whatever it is you love to do, do it, and do it while you build your business. Work toward becoming a better version of yourself to become a better person for others to be around. Become someone who leads by example. You will not regret it.

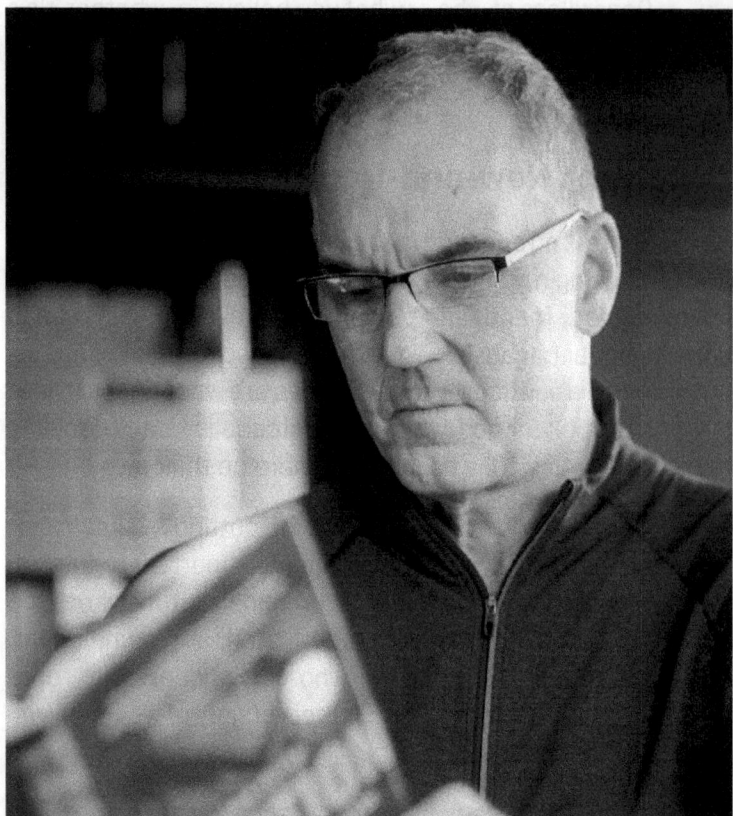

Taking the Next Step

There's a reason that I put the complacency and self-care chapter with the foundations of your business. Ensuring your health is sustainable is a critical part of building a sustainable business. Once you know your business is healthy and does not require all your time and energy, you are ready to replicate it. There is no sense in trying to do this if it will kill you. Make your self-care a priority. Avoid falling into complacency. When you have your health and well-being built into the sound foundation of your business, you are ready to take the next step. In the next chapter, I'll share how we grew our business and reach by replicating our business model.

CHAPTER 6
Replicating the Business Model

*There are no secrets to success. It is the result of preparation,
hard work, and learning from failure.*

— Colin Powell

In 2015, my son Jeffrey and I decided the asbestos removal division at ABK needed to go out on its own, with it having the legs to be a standalone company. Jeffrey took the lead at spearheading this new niche opportunity, and I asked my oldest son Byron, who was an accountant, if he was interested in being a part of the journey.

I remember them assuring me: "Dad, we just need your help getting it up and running. You have so much experience putting the processes and procedures in place to run a successful business, but we'll handle the day-to-day stuff." They were right. I knew how to make this business successful because I had already done it several times. I could learn from the mistakes I made in the past and implement the systems I knew to be successful. I felt I was finally in a good position to create something else again. And this time, with my two sons. What father wouldn't want to seize that opportunity?

By the end of 2015, Northern Hazard Solutions Inc. was born. And this time, I promised myself it wouldn't take more than two decades to get it right.

Northern Hazard Solutions Inc., The Mold & Asbestos Abatement Company

Northern Hazard Solutions Inc., branded as NorHaz, grew out of ABK when it was wearing too many hats. About three-quarters of the way through ABK, the government announced that any build pre-1990 needed asbestos testing in drywall. During this time, the awareness of asbestos was going through the roof. When people became aware of the side effects after exposure, they wanted it removed from their homes and buildings as soon as possible. So, out of sheer necessity, ABK began doing asbestos testing and removal.

However, with a team of people focusing on restoration and hundreds of projects on the go, it became increasingly difficult for the staff to keep up with the workload. They now had to deal with the government and insurance companies to ensure the process of removing asbestos was correct and safe, and it just ended up being too much work for them. We couldn't handle it any longer at ABK: It had become another animal to tackle.

That's why we, as a team, had the incredible idea to create a new company that focused on asbestos abatement. The company was split four ways: I put the systems, processes, and procedures in place. Jeffrey handled the operations. Byron handled the finances. The fourth partner, Dean, ran an asbestos company for another restoration company for years, and was ecstatic when I approached him with the idea of partnering with us. He was best suited for the project management division.

With a group of well-educated and experienced professionals running it, I knew NorHaz would thrive. The industry, recognition, and need for professionals were also growing, and the business model had been proven at ABK. The niche of asbestos abatement was up-and-coming, so we could take that bull by the horns and ride it. The timing was right, the right people were in place, and it was a go. The four of us became equal partners, and as it grew, they did most of the work, and I became a silent partner. I was making money without even doing much work.

NorHaz grew so quickly because it was a much simpler business model. Our method of assessment and removal was efficient and did not involve as many moving parts. As it grew, we added mold and lead abatement to this list of jobs we could do. Then, we started working for ABK clients, commercial companies, and private residential work because we got a hydro-vac trailer to extract the asbestos-containing insulation in people's attic spaces. These were more lucrative jobs, taking us to new levels of success.

In five years, we had taken NorHaz from a thought to millions of dollars in revenue.

Implementing the Right Brand, People, and Systems

Jeff's sons, Jeffrey and Bryon

Replicating the business model at NorHaz was almost foolproof because I knew we needed the right brand, people, and systems from the beginning. And the best part was I already knew what to do. We could make decisions fairly quickly because of my experience and the combined expertise of Jeffrey, Bryon, and Dean. With all of our brains combined, it's no wonder we were able to grow as exponentially and rapidly as we did in just a few years.

In its earlier years, we had one location but several fully-stocked trucks that allowed the team to travel to different locations in surrounding areas. We knew the positions we needed to get the job done effectively, with project managers managing their jobs and their own set of labourers, handling their clientele, and providing impeccable customer service. We knew exactly who should be on the leadership team—from management to operations, to marketing and finance. We utilized a fully digital record-keeping system, allowing us to go paperless and facilitate a streamlined documentation process.

Because of our seamless execution, our reputation grew and word of mouth spread like wildfire. We already had such an astounding reputation at ABK, so clients who'd previously worked with us wanted to jump at the opportunity to work with NorHaz. People loved working with us because we made them feel we could do the job well. There was never any doubt, any fear, any hesitation when it came to our customers. They knew if they hired NorHaz, they would have a solution to their problem by the end of the day.

NorHaz is a flawless example of what can happen to your business when you model its foundation properly from the onset. No wonder it's the leading advice in every top business book today. Every successful business, from boutiques to national franchises to global corporations, follows the same template to achieve success. They've mastered the power of branding. They've hired the right people for the right seats. They've implemented systems to maximize efficiency and streamline results. These businesses are ready to evolve with the ever-changing times and handle growing pains with deliberate execution. They keep up with technological advances and train their teams to do the same. They provide outstanding customer service to produce referring machines. They have people working on the business, in and for the business. They desire to be the best in their industry, and the results are undeniable.

Deciding the Right Time to Sell

The success of NorHaz and ABK was overwhelming, increasingly so that after decades of impeccable business growth and development, we collectively decided it was time to sell. The investment we would need to make to grow the team to keep up with the demand was not something that could be ignored; its exponential growth meant we needed a whole other level of executives in place to keep it afloat and thriving, and that was something neither of us were ready to commit to. It became painstakingly obvious that it was time for us to relinquish our shares and sell the company to someone ready for that massive undertaking. So, five years from its inception, we sold NorHaz. At the same time, I decided to let go of ABK, who was also experiencing a similar trajectory.

By September 2020, ABK and NorHaz were bought out by a private equity firm that had a large portfolio of restoration companies. This company could give them the devotion needed to expand beyond small local businesses to a massive industry-dominated empire. Today, ABK Restoration continues to grow its three locations, while Norhaz has expanded to nine locations across British Columbia. They remain the leading companies in fire and flood restoration and asbestos abatement in the province.

In the next chapter, I'll walk you through the steps I took to sell my companies for millions of dollars and what you need to know to ensure this process is smooth and seamless so you can walk away with millions in the bank.

Selling the Businesses for Millions

Your ability to do well in life depends on your ability to sell others on the things in which you believe.

— Grant Cardone

At the beginning of 2019, I had offers from three companies interested in buying ABK and NorHaz. I'd spent 30 years building ABK from the ground up and five years helping my business partners do the same for NorHaz. Both ABK and NorHaz were growing exponentially and quickly; we knew we would need to invest a lot of time, money, and energy to develop another level of the leadership team, hire more project managers and technicians, and invest in more equipment to keep up with the level of growth both companies were experiencing. Could we have done it? Absolutely. But our desire to do so was a different story.

Here's the thing: I was at a point in my life where I had already proven I could accomplish these goals. Whatever challenges were in my way, I could face them. The rest of the team could, too. But as tenacious, hungry, and eager people, we knew we had other opportunities elsewhere that we wanted to focus on. If three companies were willing to pay top-dollar for our companies, maybe it was time to take one of them up on it.

In my head, the decision was easy. Everything had been taken care of at ABK. I could have easily walked away from it because of the outstanding team I had in place who were doing everything. I was solely there to put out the odd fire, but as the years progressed, there were very few to tend to. Our accounts were impeccable, our team was sharp, our work was flawless, and our customers were happy. I wasn't needed, so I put my efforts into helping out the partners at NorHaz. When my work was done there, I wasn't needed there either. I had mastered this process and noticed that the teams could take it over seamlessly once I got the ball rolling. It's almost like I had quit years ago without telling anybody. The challenge ended, and by early 2020, I was eager to take on something else.

I scheduled a meeting with Jeffrey, Bryon, and Dean to tell them about the companies interested in buying us out. After deliberating back and forth, we concluded that none of us wanted to continue to do this in the long term. Each of us had individual goals we wanted to fulfill, and the shares we would get from selling the businesses would be pretty life-changing. That is one of the reasons you grow a business in the first place, right? Let's set aside fulfillment and helping others and grow something from scratch from the ground up. We all want to make money and afford our desired lifestyles.

Breaking Down the Selling Process

When we ultimately decided the time was right and would sell, this process was pretty easy for us since we had large corporations knocking on our door to acquire us. Why?

Because they knew of our reputation. They understood that if they were to buy us out, there would be little they would have to do because everything was already set up perfectly for them. Successful businesses want to acquire other successful businesses—that's just a fact. Every business owner knows how much work it takes for a business to thrive. So unless that is their objective, most larger corporations won't want to touch it.

But the fact is, you want to sell to someone who you know will carry on the brand's legacy, not one who will run it into the ground. After several business meetings with several prospective corporations, we ultimately decided on a company. Still, the deal fell through due to the peak of the COVID-19 pandemic and the uncertainty of the economy. Another company stepped in around the same time, but it wasn't a good fit. Finally, we landed on selling to a private equity firm in the same space. They were based in Vancouver and were doing a lot of work for the same insurance company as us. I had always heard great things about them and knew they would be a great fit to carry the torch. With them taking on the fire and flood services and asbestos removal, they would be a great option for our current and new customers to work with. The process was ultimately quite simple because all of our books were up to date (that's why it pays to have a fantastic bookkeeper and an accountant who is up to date on tax laws). This makes the due diligence process a walk in the park since there are no surprises when examining our financial records.

The Earn-Out Process

One of my primary motivations for exiting was the ability to receive payment promptly without committing to an extended earn-out period. It aligned with my desire to leave the business without lingering obligations. Even today, while some of my colleagues still hold shares in the company, I successfully navigated a clean exit, avoiding the need for prolonged involvement.

An earn-out typically involves an agreed-upon period, often two years, during which the seller remains with the company to facilitate a smooth transition. When contemplating the prospect of a two-year earn-out, the risks become apparent. Depending on how the contract is structured, it could mean fluctuating payments based on business performance. But what if the numbers don't meet expectations, leading to reduced payouts? Could they manipulate the situation?

Given my understanding of the venture capital company's focus on geographically successful businesses, I wanted a straightforward deal without contingencies. The venture capital company had been focused on acquiring successful businesses strategically covering the northern part of British Columbia. I recognized that the areas that our three locations serviced provided an opportunity for seamless integration into their plan.

Although a broker approached us initially, I decided we did not need one. Because of my son Bryon's expertise as an accountant and our excellent financial team, we were able to mediate the deal ourselves. With clean books, the transition unfolded seamlessly. I always stress the importance of keeping clean books with the business owners I coach.

The Valuation and Negotiation Process

Handling the valuation wasn't solely Bryon's responsibility; it was a collaborative effort. We exchanged numbers, tweaked figures, and eventually settled on an agreeable price. After reaching a consensus, the due diligence process involving both accountants proceeded smoothly.

The sale was finalized in November 2020. Although I could walk away immediately, I stayed on for a while as part of the transition.

Ensuring a Clean Balance Sheet

Preparation is critical for those considering selling their companies. While due diligence may seem complex, having clean and organized financial records significantly expedites the process. Negotiating a deal requires careful consideration, and aligning on a fair valuation is imperative.

The first crucial step is to ensure your balance sheet is clean. This means no hidden agendas or unresolved issues. If there's bad debt or anything unusual, it's essential to address it. Keeping your books up to date and being transparent is key. If you're considering selling, having clean financial records can significantly impact your company's value.

Some may decide to sell when they realize the business isn't for them, but waiting until the last minute might impact the numbers. Some actions may have a quick impact on the books. For instance, letting go of a high-paying employee the previous year could have positively influenced profits. But this is not the kind of practice that will lead to a confident and easy exit. Consulting with your accountant early on can provide valuable insights if you're unsure about selling.

Navigating the Valuation Process

My accountant directed me to an appraiser who could evaluate the company. After charging a fee, the appraiser thoroughly examined our books, market trends, and our business's long-term performance. The evaluation involved discussions and clarifications on any discrepancies. The final valuation considered both historical performance and future projections. While the initial evaluation came from the appraiser (and it was significantly lower than what we sold for), we realized that knowing our company's geographical strengths and goodwill was crucial. We decided on a value based on our understanding of the market and the positive reputation we had built.

Using a Broker vs. Self-Negotiation

When dealing with a broker, they take a significant percentage of the deal. Using a broker doesn't make sense if you've got clean books, good financial people, and you know what you're worth. If you're uncertain, a good broker can always help you reach your end goal. They will save you a lot of time and effort during this process.

Understanding the Business Niche

Factors like global warming influenced the market's attractiveness in the restoration business. While restoration companies may experience a downturn during less severe weather, the niche remains appealing due to increased incidents like burst pipes during extreme temperatures.

Strategic moves play a vital role in considering the sale of a business. Understanding your industry, competitors, and where you fit in is crucial. I recognized this when contemplating the sale of our restoration company. It's not just about selling; it's about finding the right fit and foreseeing potential buyers.

In our case, I observed the big players in the Valley and strategized. We decided that if a large company were to purchase us, it would be because we were geographically well-placed, privately owned, and with no affiliations. Buying us out would be a straightforward acquisition, providing the purchaser with a geographic stronghold. I knew that this would provide us with significant negotiating power.

Understanding the Market

Understanding the market value of your business is crucial. I engaged an appraiser who considered our books, market trends, and long-term performance. Valuations involve a dialogue, ensuring both parties understand the reasoning behind the figures. In our case, knowing our geographical strengths and goodwill influenced our perceived value. I insisted on a valuation higher than the one provided by the broker, which ended up working in our favour.

The Power of Doing It Right

Doing things right is foundational. This goes beyond the sale—it's about the entire business journey. Paying taxes and suppliers and adhering to ethical practices contribute to a stellar infrastructure.

Determining the selling price involves a thoughtful process. Considering my vocation, I decided what I wanted for my boys and myself. It's a personal decision tied to your financial needs and life stage. If you aim to exit, plan for it a year or two in advance. Assess your company every six months, making adjustments. Consider a two-year plan as buyers scrutinize quarterly performance.

Start your business with an end goal in mind, pondering how long you'll stay. I realized the importance of this mindset too late with my first venture, treating it like a piggy bank to fund other ventures. Plan strategically; you could optimize your business's worth by anticipating industry shifts and potential expansions.

Negotiation Dynamics

Negotiating the sale involves effective communication. We had met with three companies that expressed explicit interest in buying us. It was a great exercise to meet with them as they helped us establish a value for the company. When our valuation suggested we could ask for more, it was grounded in confidence. Strong recent performance and growth allowed us to negotiate based on solid numbers. Be transparent and assertive about your company's value.

Adaptability is crucial. Industry trends and the potential to diversify matter. Explore if your business model is relevant for the future and if it allows for additional services. For example, vent cleaning could be an add-on for restoration companies. Researching competitors and industry trends can help identify potential areas for expansion.

Safety and Compliance Impact

Safety and compliance are significant, especially in industries like asbestos removal. Showcase adherence to safety rules. NorHaz was always exacting regarding safety and handling asbestos, which always put us on the radar as a great company. In British Columbia, recent changes necessitated licensing for asbestos removal. Embracing this change early on was a no-brainer for us, so it did not surprise me to see NorHaz contributing to an article in WorkSafe magazine on the subject after I had exited. Prioritize safety, follow regulations, and highlight your commitment to compliance. Many companies struggled because they were not on top of the compliance regulations. This made NorHaz a desirable choice.

Leverage successes for marketing. Being featured in industry publications boosts credibility. For instance, the WorkSafe magazine highlighting NorHaz's commitment to safety can be shared on social media platforms for broader visibility. Showcase not only profitability but also a commitment to industry standards.

Negotiating Value and Business Models

Determining the selling price involves smart negotiations. Knowing your business' value versus what someone sees in the books is crucial. Factors like geography and potential buyers play a role. It's not just about selling your company; it's about understanding the dynamics and making strategic decisions.

Each business is unique. For instance, a smaller plumbing company selling to a larger one might create a win-win situation. You work for them, get paid, and smoothly exit. Not everyone sells businesses at the level I did, and there are diverse exit strategies to explore.

Client-Base Acquisition

Some companies buy others solely for their client base. It's a way of assimilating and expanding quickly. Our restoration companies were bought for a strategic client extension. Having a strong client base, especially with insurance companies, can make your business an attractive choice.

The difference lies in the business model. When a company is bought solely for its client base, assimilation may involve bringing the customers into the purchaser's operation. Despite the acquisition, our operations remained intact in our case because the buyer was building its strength geographically to extend their reach. Strategic positioning matters. In our case, geography played a significant role. Profitability was a plus, but the geographical fit was equally crucial. Their plans for expansion and potential future sales to larger entities or insurance companies were instrumental in their acquisition strategy.

For me, it was time to move on to my life goals outside of work. I did not want to stay on for an extended period, and I made sure that the deal we negotiated allowed for that. I like to say that I resigned 10 years ago and didn't tell anyone. It wasn't that I'd given up or lost interest. I had designed myself out of the process on purpose. The time had finally come for me to move on to life after ABK.

Jeffrey, Byron, Dean, and Jeff toasting the sale of ABK and NorHaz

CHAPTER

Navigating Life After Selling

A man can succeed at almost anything for which he has unlimited enthusiasm.

— Charles Schwab

Most business owners who sell their businesses reap the benefits of their newfound time and money by spending it however they please. However, I sold ABK and NorHaz during the peak of the pandemic, during a time when the entire world was isolated inside their homes and when people had nothing to do and no one to see. It was quite an interesting experience, to say the least, considering I'd spent my entire life working and was looking forward to having the time to do whatever I wanted. But, with everything shut down, I was forced to figure out new things that could bring joy to my life and allow me to still feel like a productive member of society.

But, as terrible as the pandemic was, it came at a pivotal time when I needed the time away in isolation to think about what I wanted in this next phase of my life. In isolation from the world around me, I thought long and hard about the answers to questions that would inherently shape my future: What do I want to do next? How do I want to spend my days? How do I want to pass my time? What is going to make me feel useful and productive? What is the thing that will feel the most rewarding? Where would my skillset best be utilized?

Coincidentally, shortly after, I received an invite from an acquaintance of mine, John Assaraf, to join the Clubhouse app, which allows members to have real-time conversations with people worldwide about various topics in virtual "rooms." It was exactly what I needed at the time. Whatever topic you could think of, Clubhouse had it. Real Estate rooms, Music rooms, Celebrity Gossip rooms, Sports rooms—you name it, there was a room for it.

Jeff McCallum, John Assaraf, and Bob Burnham

I started attending this room called Our Mindset, created by Silicon Valley Angel Investor Manny Fernandez. I was so elated by the experience that I became one of the room's moderators, discussing ways to help business owners become successful, increase their income, elevate their mindset, and be set up for long-term success. At the onset of its success, we had about 1000 people listening. We interviewed dozens of successful entrepreneurs and big names, from Grant Cardone, and Glenn Morshower to the Dupont family, Denis Waitley, and John Assaraf. We even got Michelle Obama at one point because Manny was so deeply invested in politics! Our Mindset room in the Clubhouse app rapidly grew in popularity and, at its peak, had 100,000 listeners.

The Our Mindset room within the Clubhouse app was a great place to sink my teeth into speaking to an audience about business growth and mindset. As the audience grew to over 100,000 members, Manny decided to create his own app, which now has over 300,000 members, where I am a speaker.

Do What You Love, and Run With It

When I joined the Clubhouse app, I thought it would be an excellent opportunity to listen to other experts discuss their experiences and learn more about business. Eventually, I became a moderator, sharing my own experiences and knowledge of business. We still do that every day, seven days a week, and we stream it on all social media apps. This is a great place for me to continue to develop my speaking and communication on many different levels with a wide international audience. Many people have sought my expertise and advice on growing or improving their businesses, and this platform is fulfilling my love for consulting and helping others.

People ultimately get into business to make money. Still, they also want to create something extraordinary, grow it to the best of their ability, and then reap the rewards of it during and after. However, much can be said about what happens after that business is no longer yours to cultivate and develop. There is something to be said about how you spend your time afterwards when you no longer invest all of your time into that particular thing. And most of the time, this period can be pretty scary and uncertain for many people. What should you now put all of your energy into? How are you going to pass the time? What will you do to lead a fulfilling life?

For me, I discovered that I wanted to spend my time consulting, which is why I wanted to write this book. But what will you do? Navigating life after selling does not have to be such a daunting experience. With your newfound money and freedom, you could do whatever you're interested in that you didn't have the time or opportunity to focus on beforehand. Maybe you want to take your experience and implement it into a new business venture that piques your curiosity. Maybe there is a new niche opportunity you can tackle that wasn't feasible years prior. Whatever it is, understand that you've put in the hours and deserve the time to figure out how you see your time being spent. Sit in it for a while. Talk to a career coach. Do some research. The opportunities are ripe for the picking.

When I started working with a career coach, she showed me that I had a real opportunity to help others with the knowledge I've acquired over the last four decades. I had a higher calling that I wanted to delve into. When it is no longer challenging, I must move on and do something else. Something that will challenge me to work towards things, learn new things, and make mistakes.

So, I created my website, jeffmccallum.com, and inserted an option where people could book 15-minute Zoom sessions with me for free. I set up social media accounts like Instagram, LinkedIn, YouTube and Facebook, where I would post daily about things I've been working on and promoting my website so people would go in and book if they needed business advice. With more exposure online, I started getting people from all walks of life asking me not only personal success questions but, of course, business questions, which ultimately told me I was going in the right direction.

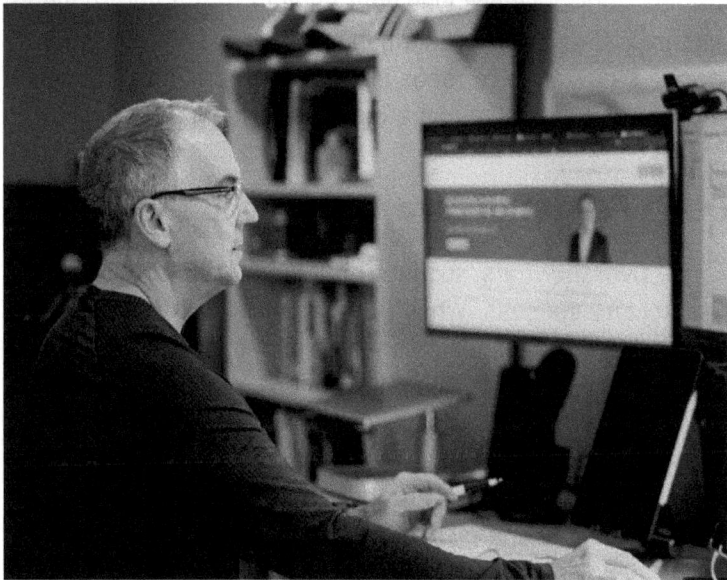

So, if you are either growing your business to sell it or are now in the phase of wanting to sell your business and restructuring your company to ensure it is ready for the send-off and are trying to decide what's next, this is your reminder to channel everything you've learned over the years and apply it to a new venture that will spark interest and ignite your soul.

Enjoy Your Time Off—You Deserve It!

While the question, "What will I do next?" after you've sold your business, I can't stress enough how important it is to schedule time for yourself and your family and friends. Take that vacation to Europe you've been planning your whole life! Read 50 books in a year if you want to! Listen to all the podcasts about gardening, music, or true crime! You've worked hard to get to where you are now, and life is meant to be enjoyed. Use that hard-earned cash and invest in your interests you didn't have time to do while building your empire. Your business was your vehicle to get you to where you are today. After investing in it and your employees for so long, it's now time to focus on your passions and the wants you've put aside to keep it afloat and thriving.

Don't Forget to Give

Over the years, so many people have contributed to my growth and success. While I attribute the law of reciprocity to much of my good fortune, I believe it is important to consciously give first and then receive. At this point in my life, it's easy for me to do well in most business ventures. My interest now is being of service to others along this path. I got what I needed from growing big ventures. Now, it's time for me to invest my energy in developing people.

CHAPTER 9
Developing Your Growth Mindset

The mind is just like a muscle—the more you exercise it,
the stronger it gets and the more it can expand.

— *Idowu Koyenikanb*

As I reflect on my journey of the last 30 years, I realize that I wouldn't have been able to accomplish all the things I did without having a growth mindset. I didn't start this way, and as you may have noticed throughout this book, I made many choices and decisions, I read lots of books, and I learned from anyone who was doing better than me. My study of successful people led me to understand that the most important factor is mindset, which is available to everyone and only embraced by a few.

The concept itself is very simple. It is up to you to find the positive in everything. Every problem holds infinite possibilities. This is very easy to say, but it can be more difficult to believe in practice. Throughout my life, by constantly honing my attitude and feeding my mind with positive thoughts, I have found opportunities everywhere, even when the rest of the world was whining and complaining.

Every chapter in this book contained valuable material about maintaining a positive mindset. It is the most critical thing you can do to be successful. This final chapter is short, but I wanted to finish with my favourite tips about mindset. These are not just feel-good sayings to post on Instagram with a nice selfie. These have been the guiding principles in my life. Everything I am most proud of has resulted from living by the following 21 principles I am about to share with you.

21 Principles to Develop a Growth Mindset

1. **Determine your goal, and make that your singular focus:** What is your goal? Are you in business as a vehicle for the lifestyle you've always dreamed of? Is it a vehicle to enter into other businesses? Do you want a small business or a large corporation? Do you have an exit in mind? Always have a plan and goals you want to achieve. This is crucial to get you to where you need to be.

2. **Business, and life itself, is just a series of decisions:** You must make several decisions in your life and business. Do the best research, speak with others who have had success before you, and make the best decision for you. You will inevitably run into problems being an entrepreneur, but be confident in your choices, practice resilience if they don't pan out the way you expected, try again, and don't be afraid to fail.

3. **Understand the difference between anxiety versus excitement:** When you have a problem or opportunity, and those inevitable butterflies start hijacking your stomach, ask yourself, "Am I excited about this opportunity, or is there something about this that is causing me to feel anxious about it?" Anything remarkable comes with that sense of excitement, but most can mistake it for anxiety.

4. Time is your most valuable commodity: Practice saying "no" more; it can be powerful. Your time is precious and should only be spent doing what you enjoy and benefit your growth and development as an entrepreneur and an individual.

5. You're in charge of your narrative: You can change your story anytime, and the possibilities are endless. If one path or narrative isn't working for you, it's never too late to try something else and cultivate a new narrative for yourself.

6. Realize that "it's all made up": People make things up as they go: Steve Jobs made up Apple computers. Howard Schultz made up Starbucks. Make your own thing and break the rules. Nobody needs to anoint you with a sword before you can do great things.

7. A niche will set you apart from others: Always consider your niche or how you could provide your specialized knowledge to the masses. This can help you stand out, reduce competition, and provide services that benefit others.

8. Everything you do in life is the result of your mindset and actions: If you go through life with a negative mindset and a crappy attitude, you're not going to get much out of this world. Try to think from an abundance and growth perspective instead of a scarcity one.

9. Powerful self-talk will help you thrive: Look at the life you've created for yourself and appreciate that you get to wake up and do the thing you love every day. Say to yourself, "I get to do this?" You can control your destiny if you let yourself believe you can.

10. Remember the phrase, "Would you rather be right or

successful?": Do you spend time defending your point on issues with others? Ask yourself, "Will arguing this point make a difference?" Even if you know the answer, it may be better to say nothing.

11. **Be kind to yourself:** We are our worst critics, so this is easier said than done. Don't compare yourself to others so intensely. Life is a journey of constant wisdom, and you're learning along the way. If you make a mistake, don't judge yourself so harshly. It's a part of the process, and that mistake can help you make leaps toward a better decision in the future. Treat yourself as you would treat others. Have an attitude of gratitude and speak positively to yourself.

12. **Manners are free:** Being kind to others costs nothing. This will take you far with your customers, employees, colleagues, and strangers.

13. **Look at things in black and white, and you'll save yourself a lot of trouble:** Sometimes, things are right or wrong. Spending too much time living in the grey zone can take you down the wrong path, causing you to overthink and prevent you from making decisions that are good for you. If you're unsure of something, find the answers from a trusted source, but ultimately, look at things objectively and see them for what they are at face value.

14. **Show up for yourself every day, as that is how you can show up for others:** Are you the type of person who walks into a room and pulls the oxygen out, or do you fill it with oxygen? Be kind to people, lead with generosity, and present the version of yourself you want people to see, and they'll enjoy being around your energy.

15. **Health is the key to success:** Your body, mind, and soul

are the most essential parts of you, and they need to be your top priority to navigate life successfully. Pay attention to your physical, emotional, mental, and spiritual well-being, and try to improve them daily.

16. **Remember the three-decision rule:** Sometimes, you're only three decisions away from greatness. What those three decisions are is entirely subjective. It only takes a few "yeses" in business to turn your life around.

17. **Continue to network for the rest of your life:** Networking is a powerful tool. It can help you grow your business, get answers to important questions, and open doors to new opportunities. Stay curious and learn from others, as they can be the ticket to a path you may not have ever anticipated.

18. **Be cautious of speculation and hearsay:** Do research, refrain from believing everything you hear, and try things out for yourself. Misinformation is prevalent in our society today, and false news can cause catastrophic events. Find credible sources and always approach things with a grain of salt.

19. **Stay mentally focused by taking action:** Clarity comes ten seconds after you put something into action.

20. **Keep practicing:** As you get better at something, you have more say in how your life unfolds.

21. **Make your own plans:** If you don't make plans for yourself, guess what others have planned for you?

These 21 principles have guided my life for well over 40 years. They have served me well and helped me do much good. Not a single day goes by where I don't find myself spouting one off to someone or another. The reason is that they work. The reason they work is because they have become part of my DNA. The way I made that happen was through repetition. I suggest you do the same if you're serious about doing well in your business. I've prepared a PDF copy you can download by scanning this QR code. Print it out and read it every day.

If you think this sounds excessive, pause and rethink. Everything you have today is a result of your thoughts. If you find me any successful person, I will find some version of repetition they use to condition their mindset for success. You can't leave this to chance. It's up to you to feed your mind with the material that shapes your dreams. Otherwise, the stuff that will creep in will poison your mindset and lead you down a path you probably don't want to go.

Have fun with these principles. I know I did, and I still do. I taught them to my sons, and we continue to use them as they build their businesses. I am so blessed to have the life I do, and I am grateful every day for the opportunities to create more good. I hope you can build a successful business and life with these principles.

Conclusion

Risk more than others think is safe. Dream more than others think is practical.

— Howard Schultz

Writing this book took a lot of digging into the past, deep contemplation, and understanding the meaning of things that may not have been apparent then. Hindsight is always 20/20. It has been wildly therapeutic and rewarding. Throughout my years in business, I've helped hundreds of people thrive in the fire and flood restoration industry. It's not glamorous and doesn't demand extensive education or skills. Many individuals I've worked with haven't come from privileged backgrounds. However, what remains consistent is the transformative power of mindset, success principles, and structured systems. Through these, I've moulded individuals who share my vision and dedication. This has been instrumental in building my businesses and realizing my dreams.

Giving back is fundamental to my philosophy. I actively participate in various groups and frequently speak about business to entrepreneurs. After these talks, people often approach me, seemingly thriving on the surface but struggling internally. Despite outward appearances, many face breakdowns in mindset, operations, or foundational business elements. However, I find these moments exhilarating because I've navigated similar challenges. By seeking guidance from mentors and asking the right questions, I've overcome obstacles and turned setbacks into opportunities.

Throughout my career, I've sought mentorship from those who have excelled beyond me. I've invested in their expertise, recognizing the value it brings to my business journey. I eagerly seek coaches who can expand my knowledge and skills. The process of learning something entirely new is invigorating to me. It's like crafting a masterpiece on a blank canvas. Today, as I consult and coach business owners, I'm honoured to share these insights. Whether offering simple advice or rebuilding from the ground up, I'm passionate about helping entrepreneurs realize their potential.

As this book evolves into other media forms—podcasts, courses, and blogs—I invite you to join me. Follow me on your preferred platform and enroll in the upcoming mini-course. If you're ready to elevate your life and business, let's connect. I'm excited to explore the endless possibilities with you. No matter your challenge, there's always a solution waiting to be seized. Together, we can build a thriving business and lead a successful life. Reach out, and let's embark on this transformative journey together.

To learn more, follow me on social media for more tips, especially regarding marketing secrets.

https://www.facebook.com/JeffSMcCallum/

https://www.instagram.com/jeffsmccallum/

https://www.linkedin.com/in/jeff-mccallum-2951798/

https://www.youtube.com/channel/UCkAj6oPRpQsC5XxAIa686PA

https://www.tiktok.com/@jeffsmccallum

https://www.threads.net/@jeffsmccallum

https://twitter.com/expertauthor1